PRIMEVAL SAINTS

PRIMEVAL SAINTS
Studies in the Patriarchs of Genesis

by James B. Jordan

Canon Press ▣ *Moscow*

James B. Jordan, *Primeval Saints: Studies in the Patriarchs of Genesis*
© 2001 by James B. Jordan
Published by Canon Press, P.O. Box 8741, Moscow, ID 83843
800-488-2034 / www.canonpress.org

06 05 04 03 02   9 8 7 6 5 4 3

Cover design by Paige Atwood Design, Moscow, ID
Cover art: Rembrandt van Rijn, Jacob Blessing of the Children of Joseph. 1656. Oil
on canvas. Stattliche Museen, Kassel, Germany.

Printed in the United States of America.

Library of Congress Cataloging-in-Publication Data

Jordan, James B., 1949
Primeval Saints: Studies in the Patriarchs of Genesis / by James B. Jordan
    cm.
Includes bibliographical references and index.
ISBN 1-885767-86-2 (pbk.)
  1. Patriarchs (Bible) I. Title.
  BS573 .J67 2001
  222'.1106-dc21

CONTENTS

INTRODUCTION   9

1 FAITH AND THANKFULNESS
   The Stories of Adam and Cain   13

2 FAITH AND WORSHIP
   The Stories of Seth and Enoch   29

3 FAITH AND REST
   The Story of Noah   41

4 FAITH AND REBELLION
   The Stories of Ham and Nimrod   51

5 FAITH AND PATIENCE
   The Story of Abraham   61

6 FAITH AND COMMUNITY
   The Story of Lot   75

7 FAITH AND TYRANNY
   The Stories of Isaac and Rebekah   85

8 FAITH AND ACCEPTANCE
   The Story of Esau   101

9 FAITH AND WRESTLING
   The Story of Jacob   107

10 FAITH AND SERVICE
   The Story of Joseph   117

11 FAITH AND THE WORLD
   The Story of Pharaoh   129

12 FAITH AND SLAVERY
   The Story of the Egyptians   141

SCRIPTURE INDEX   151

For my sons
Dale and Douglas

INTRODUCTION

The book of Genesis contains the Bible in a nutshell. It records the beginnings (geneses) of all things, and everything that happens later in the Bible is an unfolding of what happens for the first time in Genesis. Because of this, the book of Genesis can and should be studied from a variety of angles, with attention paid to a variety of themes.

Yet, above all these themes is the overarching notion of beginnings and what develops out of beginnings. In the very first chapter we see God create the world, and then out of this beginning develops one good thing after another, with each new thing "begetting" in a broad way the next new thing as the Spirit works with the world. Then Genesis records a series of epochs in early history, each of which is "begotten" by the one that precedes it, and each of which transforms the old into something new.

Similarly, fathers and sons (or daughters) are continually in view in Genesis. We see this not only in the genealogies (which some wit has called "the begatitudes"), but also in the attention paid to Adam and his sons, Noah and his sons, Abraham and his sons, Isaac and his sons, and Jacob and his sons. In each case the son is called to carry forward the faithfulness of his father in new ways, becoming a new kind of person, and advancing beyond his father as "new occasions teach new duties."[1]

Fascinating as such themes are, our interest in this book is simpler. We are concerned with the heroes of the city of God. Our focus is limited to individual people, their faith in God, and what that faith meant for them.

---

[1] As human beings are images of God, what Genesis shows about fathers and sons is an implicit revelation of God the Father and God the Son.

Heroism can be a dangerous idea. In the pagan world, hero-ism means pretty much the opposite of what it means in the Bible, but Christians too often get their ideas of heroism from the pagans. A reading of pagan literature, such as Homer's *Iliad,* reveals to us that for the pagan, the hero is consumed with his own honor and that of his family and society. He acts on that honor by killing other people and by being killed in some hon-orable fashion. These two notions, honor and death, are inverted in the Bible.[2]

The Christian is never to be motivated by a sense of his own honor, but rather by the honor of Christ. If pride was Satan's original sin, humility and patient faith are the Christian's pri-mary duty. The Christian casts his own honor in the dust so that God may be honored, knowing that God and God alone can give him true honor. The Christian, thus, lives by obedi-ence and submission, not by pride and honor and nobility. The Christian lives by something outside himself—God's com-mands, and not by something inside himself—his sense of honor.

Honor is our sense of self-worth, of self-importance. Since we are created as the very images of God Himself, we are in-deed worthy and important. But our sense of our worth must never come from ourselves. It must always come from God's calling us to be His.

The pagan hero acts to preserve his honor from shame and disgrace, but the Christian hero, like Jesus, is willing to take up a cross, even though the public exposure of nakedness that the cross entails is monumentally shameful.

The pagan hero acts to preserve his name and reputation; the Christian hero is willing to endure slander and to ask God and God alone for eventual vindication.

---

[2]An excellent discussion of the Homeric (and pagan) ideals of honor and heroism is found in Peter J. Leithart, *Heroes of the City of Man: A Christian Guide to Select Ancient Literature* (Moscow: Canon Press, 1999).

In a duel or war, like that which Homer recounts in the *Iliad*, the pagan hero kills to preserve his name and his honor.

The pagan stands his ground, guarding his own rights, but the Christian guards only the rights of God and, in doing so, he is willing to give up his own things in order to preserve peace. Thus, when the Philistines kept seizing Isaac's wells, Isaac simply moved on to another place and dug another well—not a very honorable response from a pagan point of view.

From the pagan point of view, Abram did not act honorably when he told Sarai to tell Pharaoh that she was his sister and not his wife. Many Christians have faulted him for this, but as we shall see, he was acting in faith to preserve God's kingdom. And God vindicated him.

The pagan seeks to save himself, to save his sense of his own honor. The believer trusts in God for salvation and even for daily bread and is willing to die rather than let God down. Thus, while the pagan seeks an honorable death full of glory, the Christian is ready for an ignominious and shameful death. We can think of Jesus Himself, of course, but in Genesis we think of Joseph. He was ready to die rather than betray God, though he was spared by Potiphar who understood what had really happened (Gen. 40).

Finally, because the pagan does not believe and trust in God's kingdom, he makes his own country and family paramount. In the *Odyssey*, all Odysseus wants to do is get home. In the *Iliad*, the heroic Hector leaves his wife and son to be enslaved rather than abandon his clan and city, despite knowing that the Trojans are in the wrong and are doomed. "My country, right or wrong" was his operating principle. But the Christian hero is willing, like Abram, to leave family and country behind to serve God.[3]

[3]An even better example is Jeremiah, who told Jerusalem to submit to Nebuchadnezzar and encouraged the people of the city to defect to Nebuchadnezzar's army. The "honor of Jerusalem" was not Jeremiah's interest, but rather the kingdom of righteousness.

In these studies we look at a number of examples of true heroism—heroism that stems from faith in God and not from any sense of personal honor. We explore different aspects of the faith to which God called various people, and how they responded.

We shall see that true faith is thankful, not proud and grasping.

We shall see that true faith worships God and is not oriented toward self.

We shall see that true faith is restful and patient, not restless and impatient.

We shall see that true faith is submissive, not rebellious.

We shall see that true faith operates in a community of the faithful, and that it trusts God when faced with tyranny and oppression.

We shall see that true faith wrestles with God for blessings, not first and foremost with men.

We shall see that true faith serves others and does not seek to lord it over them.

And we shall see that the fruit of true faith is blessing and salvation to the world.

1   FAITH AND THANKFULNESS

The Stories of Adam and Cain

The first chapter of Genesis tells us that after God made everything else and set up everything the way He wanted it to be, He then made man. He said, "Let us make man in our image, according to our likeness; and let them rule over the fish of the sea and over the birds of the heavens and over the cattle and over all the earth, and over every creeping thing that creeps on the earth" (Gen. 1:26).

We Christians are so used to reading this verse that we often miss its full impact. In fact, what is said here almost defies belief. Why? Because we are said to be created in the image of the God who made the world in verses 2-25 of Genesis One. God had made the world, and now He commissions man to take it over. But the man He designs for this task is nothing less than His own very image and likeness. It is only when we see just how wonderful and amazing man is that we can appreciate the magnitude of the Fall and the greatness of redemption.

The Glory of Man

Let us survey the earlier verses of Genesis to get an idea of what this new creature—man—is like. There we find that God caused light to shine upon a dark world, so that He could see all of it down to the last detail; then he began to work with it. That is what man is like. That is the kind of understanding God's image is created to have.

God laid hold of a formless world and gave it form. That is what man is like. That is the kind of world-shaping thing man will do.

God laid hold of an empty world and filled it. That is what man is like. That is the kind of productivity man will have.

God reorganized whole oceans and planted vegetation; He established whole ecologies. That is the kind of thing man will do.

God flung the sun, moon, and stars into space. "Could it be," wondered the angels who heard God speak in Genesis 1:26, "that this *man* will even do such things as this?"

Such is the import of the statement that man is made in God's image. Man is not a worm, but a son of the King (Lk. 3:38), not a bit player on the stage of history, but captain of the whole of God's earthly creation.

Additional wonders concerning man are seen in Genesis 2, where we read about the Garden of Eden and the first man's tasks there. "Then Yahweh God took the man and put him into the Garden of Eden to cultivate it and keep it" (Gen. 2:15). Two tasks are set out here: to cultivate or beautify the world and to keep or guard it.

First of all, God told Adam to beautify the world, starting with the garden as his first project. He was to "dress" or "cultivate" it. Adam was to take the raw materials he found in the garden and work with them in order to enhance the garden. By reworking the garden he would beautify it further, eventually transforming the whole world into the glorious city of God.

Before Adam could begin to rework the garden, he would have to study and understand it. His *scientific investigations* would be the foundation for his *artistic endeavors*, just as God's light preceded His actions. The more he learned about the acidity of soil, the better gardener man would become. The more he knew about the chemical composition of oils, the better painter he would become. The more he studied geometry, the better builder he would become. The more he understood himself, the better man he would become.

Adam would need help to do his task, and the animals would be his helpers. They would pull his plows, contribute wool to his garments, and give eggs for his table. Beyond providing these services, however, they would behave in ways that would teach Adam about himself. For example, by observing the habits of the ants, he would learn to be provident (Prov. 6:6-8). So the animals would help Adam understand himself and the world and assist him in glorifying it.

The first wisdom Adam acquired stemmed from observing that the animals came in pairs. Each animal had a mate uniquely fitted for it. For Adam, however, there was no helper specially fitted for him. From these observations Adam learned that his world-changing tasks were not to be performed by himself alone, without help. Rather, the human enterprise was to have a social dimension: Men would need women to help them, and beyond that, men would have to form larger social organisms in order to accomplish larger projects. It is not good for men to be alone (Gen. 2:18).

What a privilege! Man was to be lord of the universe under God's guidance, second only to God Himself in governing all things within the earthly creation. As great as this privilege was, however, it was not Adam's highest and most amazing glory.

Second, God entrusted Adam with the protection of His Garden. The word "keep" actually means "guard" or "protect," and it was Adam's duty to guard the garden against intruders. Protecting the garden from other would-be rulers meant offering it to God, affirming that it was God's Garden. To grasp the full weight of this we need to consider that the Garden of Eden was not simply a patch of ground. It was also God's holy sanctuary, the place of His earthly throne. Like the Tabernacle and the Temple later on, the garden was the place where God would meet with men and hold court. It was nothing less than the throne of God that Adam was called upon to guard. When Adam failed to do so, the cherubim were brought in to carry out the task (Gen. 3:24).

Consider the greatness of the task entrusted to Adam. After all, a king does not entrust the protection of His palace to just anyone. Only his most trusted and competent servants are given this task. The cherubim who took Adam's place were certainly glorious and terrifying creatures, yet it was man to whom the task was originally given. The cherubim were God's second choice. "In man We trust," said the Lord as He gave the keys of the kingdom to Adam. "Guard this Garden and everything in it. Guard your wife, and guard your own heart. Keep My palace holy."

To show him what it means to guard the garden, God arranged for another animal to approach Adam and Eve. There was nothing subtle or complicated about the serpent's assault on the garden. "God is a liar," he said, contradicting the word of God pointblank. The serpent did not directly attack Adam, but Eve. Adam, as guard, had the responsibility to protect the garden and his wife, and thus to rebuke Satan. He was to stand as warrior and priest to defend the very sanctuary of God. There is no higher calling.

Eden with its Garden was situated on a mountain or plateau. We know this because four rivers flowed out of it, and rivers only flow downstream (see also Ezek. 28:13-14). In the Bible, God frequently meets with men on mountaintops. We can think of Mount Moriah, where Abraham offered Isaac; Mount Sinai, where God met with Moses and the elders of Israel; Mount Zion, where God built His City; Mount Carmel, where God defeated the prophets of Baal; the Mount on which Jesus preached His great Sermon; and Calvary Hill, where Jesus was elevated as dying King.

Who gets to stand on this Holy Mountain? Who stands at the top of the world, right under heaven itself? Who takes the highest station, and is able to survey the whole world from the heights? Is it the lion or the ox? Is it the cherub or the seraph? No, it is man; it is Adam.

With Adam God speaks as Father to son. It is Adam to whom the world is given; he is commissioned to transform it from glory to glory. It is Adam who has the privilege of guarding the earthly throne of God from His satanic adversaries.

God created the raw material of the world and then brought it out of formlessness and emptiness over the course of six days. God initiated the project, and then He turned it over to Adam. Adam's task was nothing less than the transfiguration of the world, repeatedly, from glory to glory. He would begin with the scientific, the task of cataloguing and naming the animals, thereby coming to grips with the world. Adam would then start to work with the created order, learning progressively more difficult tasks, engaging in progressively more magnificent undertakings. There was flax to be spun into thread and made into clothing. There were dyes to be discovered to add color and glory to the clothing. There was gold to be mined and made into jewelry and other beautiful objects. There were four rivers to be followed to the four corners of the world, with ever new prospects for dominion and glory. And who knows, perhaps there were even the rocky shores of the planets and the fiery hearts of the stars to be subdued for man's use to the glory of God.

The task was limitless—with ever more complex projects, ever more magnificent undertakings. And as Adam and his posterity undertook to change the earth to God's glory, they themselves would also change, growing and maturing from glory to glory.

Greater projects would require greater time and planning. As he matured, Adam's vision would stretch beyond projects of a mere day or week, and he would begin to plan long-term endeavors. His heroic task of world-transformation would take on an "epic" quality, extending over years and even centuries. He and his descendants would come to see themselves as part of God's great design for history, with each contributing his or her part to the tapestry of universal glorification.

Such was the glory and destiny of man when he was created. Reflecting on this, David wrote, "When I consider Your heavens, the work of Your fingers, the moon and the stars, which You have ordained: What is man, that You take thought of him? And the son of man, that You care for him?" (Ps. 8:3-4). The moon and the stars are great and wondrous things and man is but a worm by comparison, so why does God bother to think on us? Rather David thinks the reverse: The moon and the stars are great and wonderful, yet God reserves His special care for man. How great must man be, since this is so!

David goes on to sing, "Yet You have made him a little lower than God, and crown him with glory and majesty! You make him to rule over the works of Your hands; You have put all things under his feet" (Ps. 8:5-6). Man is created as God's very image, just a little lower than God Himself, yet man's glory does not stop there. God will crown him with more. Man would start with children's tasks, but then God would add to him nothing less than dominion over all His creation!

Having looked at man's privilege and greatness, let us now look more closely at man's world-transforming task.

The Pattern of World-Transformation

God could have made the world instantaneously, or He could have done it over the course of six billion years. He could have taken six seconds, or six millennia. The fact that He chose to take six days is significant, for His sole declared purpose in doing so was to set a pattern for man, His image.[4] The world was designed for man, and God's actions in building up the world are prototypes of human actions in continuing to build up and glorify the world, transforming the raw materials of the garden

---

[4] This is stated in Exodus 20:10–11, where man is told to work six days and rest on the seventh because that is what God did. See James B. Jordan, *Creation in Six Days: A Defense of the Traditional Reading of Genesis One* (Moscow: Canon Press, 1999).

and the rest of the world into the perfected beauty of the New Jerusalem, from glory to glory.

God's original creation of the heavens and the earth out of nothing is unique, and man cannot copy it. (We say "out of nothing" because God did not make the world out of His own being or out of any already-existing stuff.) From that point on, however, God acts in ways that man can copy. He brings light to darkness, gives form to the shapeless, names the unnamed, and apportions the restructured world to various kingdoms. Man as God's image copies these acts of illuminating, restructuring, naming, and distributing. We can summarize God's activity in Genesis 1:2-2:4 as a five-fold sequence of actions.

First, God takes hold of the creation. This is expressed by the phrase "And God said." God does not need hands to work, and He lays hold on things solely by the power of His Word and of His Spirit, who is the breath or out-speaking of His inner Word. Man images this aspect of the Divine work when he lays hold on any created thing in order to begin to work with it. Like God, man cannot work with anything until he has names, words, to put on what he is doing. God thinks and then puts forth His Breath to perform His actions. Similarly, the image of God thinks and then acts.

Second, God restructures the creation. This is particularly in focus in the first three days of the creation, wherein God *separates* light from darkness, waters above from waters below, land from sea. The world, already glorious in that it reflects God's glorious Person, is rendered even more glorious in the course of time by being broken down and restructured, so that at the end of each stage the world is "good," with still greater goodness to come.

Men continually and inescapably image this restructuring action of God. If I remove a book from my shelf, I have broken down the original form of my room and restructured it. If I dig up ore from the ground and heat it so as to separate gold from dross, I am restructuring. This act of restructuring is what we generally think of as work in the strict or narrow sense.

Third, God distributes His work. This is particularly apparent in the last three days, during which God gives the firmament to the sun, moon, and stars, the sea to fishes, the land to birds and animals, and all things to men. This act of distribution follows naturally after the work of transforming. After I have made something I can do one of three things with it. I can keep it for myself, I can give it away, or I can trade it for the work of someone else.

Fourth, God evaluates His work. This is noted repeatedly by the phrase "God saw what He had made and it was good," climaxing at the end: "God saw all that He had made and it was very good." Evaluation always comes before consumption or full enjoyment. Before eating there is tasting. When a mother makes a soup and distributes a bowl to each member of the family, the first taste elicits an evaluation. "Well, how do you like it?" she asks. That question comes not at the end of the meal but after the first sampling of it.

Fifth, God enjoys His work. God's sabbath rest on the seventh day was not apart from the creation; it was in it. God's temple is always set up in the midst of the world—think of the Tabernacle in the center of the Israelite camp and the Temple in the center of the land of promise. Having tasted His work and finding it good, God relaxed and enjoyed it. Similarly, if the soup tastes good, we enjoy a whole bowl of it, and maybe a second helping.

These five simple actions are as ordinary as they are inescapable. It is, or should be, encouraging and invigorating to realize that imaging God does not necessarily involve performing great, earth-shattering acts. It can be accomplished simply through carrying out very ordinary activities. For instance, when I give you a glass of water:

1. I *take hold* of a glass in the cabinet.
2. I *restructure* the cabinet by removing the glass. Just as God separated the waters above from the waters below by putting "firmament" between them, so I separate one glass from the rest, putting space between them.
1a. I also take hold of the faucet.
2b. I separate water from the pipe into the glass, dividing water from water, restructuring the water. I now have a new thing: a glass of water.
3. I *distribute* the glass of water to you.
4. You *evaluate* the water. It might taste bad if the faucet had not been used for a week and I failed to run the water out of the pipe first. Or it might taste fine.
5. Assuming you judge the water to be good, you *enjoy* it by drinking more of it.

Such simple, mundane actions constantly and unavoidably imitate God's actions in the building of the world. Thus, every calling in life, indeed every action in life, has immeasurable dignity.

Because all men, whether true believers or renegades, constantly imitate God in their work, it cannot be in the area of works where the final distinction between the righteous and the wicked is found. Rather, it is the attitude or faith that accompanies these works that makes the difference.

This requirement of right faith is set out in Genesis 2 and 3 and is seen in God's placing an additional step in man's performance of this five-fold sequence of actions. That additional step is the *giving of thanks,* a conscious act of self-submission to God, affirming that He is the One who set up the conditions for human labor and also affirming that He does all things well. This act of thanksgiving is placed immediately after the first step of "taking hold," before the act of "restructuring." While all our actions are to be invested by a spirit of thanks, an act of thanks is sometimes to be performed at this point in the sequence.

What is thanksgiving? The giving of thanks is a rendering of praise and an affirmation of dependence upon someone else. A person does not thank himself; God did not thank Himself when He made the world. That would be absurd. When, however, I thank you for something, I am acknowledging that you have done something for me (acknowledging dependence), and expressing gratitude (not resentment).

Romans 1:21, speaking of all men (and especially of Adam and Eve), says "for even though they knew God, they did not glorify Him as God, or *give thanks.*" Man was created on the sixth day of creation week. He was made in the middle of the day, after the animals were made. Before that sixth day was over, God brought various animals to Adam for him to name. The next day was the sabbath, the time when Adam was to come before God and give thanks, glorifying God as God and offering God's Garden back to Him.

It is important to reflect on what it meant for Adam to name the animals. This was not a work of restructuring. To put a name on something is a way of laying hold on it (step 1). We cannot deal with things we cannot name. Thus, it was not labor in the strict sense for Adam to name the animals. Rather, Adam was simply taking hold of the creation.[5]

Before beginning to work with the creation, Adam was to give thanks to God, affirming His sovereignty. In other words, Adam was not to give thanks to God empty-handed. Rather, it was with God's creation in his hands that Adam was to render thanks to God. This involved the dedication of his *future* works to God: Adam's future works would involve moving the

[5] After He had restructured the world, God gave the results *new* names (God called the firmament heaven, the dry land earth, etc.). Adam would give new names to new things after he had made them. His first act, though, was to *recognize* what God had already made, and thereby lay hold on it. He was not giving new names to the animals, but recognizing and describing them as God had made them.

creation from glory to glory by restructuring and redistributing it. Adam's six-fold rite for life was as follows:

1. Adam was to lay hold on the cosmos.
2. Before working with it, Adam was to give thanks to God for His gift of the cosmos. By doing this, Adam would be offering God's world to Him, apart from human works. This prayer would be an act of faith apart from works (Eph. 2:8–10).
3. Adam would then break down and restructure that portion of the cosmos within his grasp.
4. Adam would then distribute his works to others. Ten percent would be given to God on the sabbath day of judgment for God's evaluation and as a way of offering the world back to God. By giving God His tithe, Adam would be making a second offering to God, this time of God's world as transformed by human works. At this point, his faith would be made manifest in his works (Jas. 2:18). The rest Adam would keep for himself, and/or distribute to others through giving or trading.
5. Adam's works would then be evaluated. Adam would evaluate his own works, and so would other people. That portion given to God would be evaluated by Him.
6. The works of the unfallen Adam would be enjoyed by all, particularly by God, for Whom they would be a savor of sweet incense.

Two aspects of this sequence of actions call for emphasis. The first is that this process takes place in time. What is "good" at an early stage of history may not still be "good" later. A drawing by a child may be evaluated as "very good" by adults, but the same crudities from the hand of an adult would not receive the same commendation. It is important to affirm this future-oriented character of the good, because it helps to explain the fact that the products of human work do not endure but are replaced by newer works as history moves along.

The second aspect of this process is that man's six-fold action is an act of glorification. Man is God's agent for the glorification of the world. The world was created glorious, but it is to become more glorious under the hand of man. "Glory" is a difficult concept to describe, but clearly it has to do with the revelation of God. We know that God is fully revealed, and thus fully glorified, in all that He has made. Yet the work of man is to reveal God even more and bring Him even more glory.

The progressive revelation and glorification of God in history does not take place by revealing what is hidden, but by transforming what is already revealed. This is the mystery of time, of growth, of history. It means something remarkable: that even in the simplest of human actions, God's glory can be enhanced and His Person revealed more fully.

Understanding that man's actions are a work of progressive transformation and glorification also gives perspective to the transitory nature of human works. The great paintings of the Reformation era are darkening and cracking with age. Many have been destroyed in wars. Of Bach's five great Passions, only two are extant. Human works do not endure over the course of time.

For this reason some have argued that human work in the creation has meaning only because it trains men: Adam himself is progressively transformed and glorified through the six-fold action. While this touches an important truth, the problem is with the word "only." By itself, the notion that human labor exists only to train men reduces the value of work to one dimension—the subjective dimension of what it means "for me." The needed objective foundation is the confession that human labor, if it is worthwhile, progressively reveals and glorifies God. Even if the artifact does not itself endure, like the crude sketches of a child, the revelation of God and the glorification of the creation are yet cumulative.

Thus, the world is transformed from glory to glory. Each generation of men builds on the heritage passed to it by previous generations. New and better buildings replace old, crumbling ones. New and better medical insights replace old and inadequate methods.

With this pattern of transformation in mind, we are able to see more clearly the nature of Adam's sin and its effects.

The Degradation of Man and the World

Sadly, this process of glorification was corrupted. The sin of Adam lay precisely at the second step of his rite. He refused to give thanks to God, because he could not do so. With the forbidden fruit in his hand (an act of taking), and intending to eat it (an act of restructuring), Adam could not give thanks to God. Thus, Adam's original sin entailed, among other dimensions, the failure to glorify God as God (by restructuring the creation along His desired lines), and the failure to give thanks (by expressing dependence upon God and gratitude for what God had given him). The six-fold action designed for man's good was corrupted. In Cain (Gen. 4) we see this fleshed out.

1. Cain laid hold of the creation, intending to restructure it into the city of man.
2. Cain did not give thanks or express dependence and gratitude to God or to anyone else.
3. Cain restructured part of the land of Nod into the wicked city of Enoch.
4. Cain distributed his work to his son and to his heirs.
5. God came down to evaluate the works of men, and He found them evil.
6. God "enjoyed" man's works by "delighting" to destroy them in the flood.

Instead of progressively glorifying the world, man's labors progressively degraded it. Instead of a process of glorification, we have a process of debasement. Instead of an increase in the revelation of God, we have an obscuring of that revelation.

Unless arrested, this process of debasement would lead to the destruction of the world. God's promise after the flood, however, was that never again would He permit the process to go that far. Rather, in man's youth God would intervene to set things right (Gen. 8:21). That restoration entailed the whole work of Jesus Christ, especially His death under God's wrath as a substitute for our sins and His resurrection as the inauguration of the transfigured Kingdom of God.

In practical terms, Jesus set at the center of His Kingdom a rite designed to restructure our thinking and to reset the course of our lives along the true lines of our calling. He did this by establishing the ritual of the Lord's Supper, a ritual that restores us to the holy six-fold action. We shall take this up in chapter two when we see look at how worship was established on the earth.

Conclusion

Adam was a newborn child. As a child, he needed the childlike faith that Jesus insists upon: simple trust and confidence in God and His authority. A child should realize that, being new on the scene, he does not know much and needs guidance. Adam took upon himself the right to decide between God and the serpent. He made himself the authority.

Thinking he was making himself wise and mature, he made himself a fool and less than a child—a beast: "For even though they knew God, they did not glorify Him as God, *or give thanks;* but they became futile in their speculations, and their foolish heart was darkened. *Professing to be wise, they became fools,* and exchanged the glory of the incorruptible God for an image in the form of corruptible man *and of birds and four-footed animals and crawling creatures*" (Rom. 1:21–23). Had Adam and

Eve focused their affections and trust on God they would have become more and more incorruptible, like Him. Instead, they focused their affections on the serpent, and they became more and more corrupted and beastlike. Men become like their gods.

Thus, man's greatness was lost. His self-esteem as a child of God was lost. His privilege of guarding the throne was lost. The reward of his labors, his glory, was lost. The modern secular humanist, like Satan, says that man is great without God. The Bible, however, teaches the only true humanism: that man's greatness—the truly heroic and epic dimensions of his life—comes from imitating God in faith.

It is through faith that we grow from glory to glory, becoming more like God. What is faith but the attitude of trust that accompanies our actions? We either trust God and become like Him or we trust something else and become like it. Faith is inescapable, and Adam trusted his own judgment rather than God's. The consequences were disastrous.

But God was faithful to man, even when man was faithless to Him, and He acted to restore humanity to Himself and to his proper glory.

2 FAITH AND WORSHIP

The Stories of Seth and Enoch

Though God cast Adam and Eve out of His Garden, He did not leave them without hope. He promised them that someday one of their descendants would destroy Satan and reopen the heavenly gates. As a sign of His promise, He slew beasts and made clothes for them (Gen. 3:21). This action on God's part contains several interrelated meanings.

First, He clothed them as beasts. They had wanted to follow the serpent, a beast, so they would be dressed as beasts as a public confession of their sin.

Second, He clothed them in "tunics." The Bible only mentions this particular garment in connection with priests and princes. On the one hand, they had become like beasts, but on the other hand, God was promising that they could still become kings and queens. When they were created as newborn babies (though mature in size and ability), they were naked, and no more ashamed than a child would be. God did not intend for them to remain naked forever, however. After all, He is robed in glory, and we see Him robing His saints in glory throughout the Bible. We can think, for instance, of the white robes of the saints, the garments of glory and beauty of the High Priest, and Joseph's special tunic (same word as in Gen. 3:21). It was gracious of God to clothe them—a promise of His good intentions.

Third, the beast had to be slain to provide the garments. This established the principle of animal sacrifice. Animal sacrifice points in two directions. One is that the beast must be put to death. In following the serpent, men made idols of beasts. In order to worship God such idols must be killed. Every time an animal was killed or sacrificed, God's people were to remember the need to crush the beast and break the idol. Dressed as beasts, Adam and Eve were to understand that they needed to kill themselves, to mortify (put to death) their sinful inclinations.

The other aspect of animal sacrifice is that the beast was a substitute for Adam and Eve. God had said that they would die the day they ate the forbidden fruit (Gen. 2:17), but God brought in a substitute instead. "It was the beast who led you to sin," God was saying, "and so I will put your sins on the beast and kill him, sparing you and giving you a second chance." All of this pointed to Jesus Christ, who, though He knew no sin, was counted as a "beast" in God's eyes and slain in our stead (2 Cor. 5:21).

In the days and years to come, as Adam and Eve wore the skins God gave them, they would meditate on these things. "We made ourselves beasts, so we dress like beasts," they would think. "But God killed the beast, and it was He who graciously gave us these clothes." But they had hope: "Someday we will change these beast-clothes for the robes of glory that we forfeited by our sin."

Cain and Abel

Cain and Abel knew these things. As firstborn Cain was given the privilege of working with vegetables, reminders of the garden. To Abel was delegated the task of laboring with animals. We read in Genesis 4:3 that "at the end of days" the two men brought sacrifices to God. The "end of days" (literally, "cut-off point of days") is some kind of sabbath time (Gen. 2:1–3), a time of offering oneself and one's works to God.

Abel followed God's principles. He brought a clean animal and laid his hands on it. "I confess that I deserve to die for my sins under God's holy death penalty," he thought, "but God has graciously consented to take this substitute instead of me. Praise and thanks to His gracious Name!" Thus Abel confessed that he was a guilty sinner but that he trusted in God. Abel killed his beast, and God was pleased.

Cain, however, refused to follow his parents' teaching. He brought vegetables, a gift—a bribe—to God. Perhaps he was too proud to exchange vegetables for one of Abel's lambs, for Cain was a man filled with pride. At any rate, he saw no need to confess that he deserved the death penalty and also no need for a substitute. Cain did not kill his beast, and God was not pleased.

God graciously spoke with Cain as a Father to His son. He encouraged him to do right. God said, "There is a beast crouching at the door of your heart, but you must kill it, as I killed beasts to clothe your parents, and as Abel killed his beast. Kill your beast, Cain! Bring the proper sacrifice, confess your sins, and I will be pleased and your countenance will be lifted up" (cf. Gen. 4:6–7). But Cain would not listen.

Instead, Cain blamed Abel for showing him up. He and Abel got into a conversation. We can imagine that Abel exhorted his brother to do right, for Jesus called Abel a prophet (Mt. 23:31, 35). In a rage, Cain slew Abel. In his heart of hearts he thought, "If God demands a sacrifice, I'll give Him one!" Like any sacrifice, the shed blood called to God, but not for mercy. Abel's blood cried out for vengeance.

Yet even here God was merciful, and instead of killing Cain, He put a mark upon him. We should see this as the original "mark of the beast," perhaps even on the forehead where Adam had sweat (Gen. 3:19). Cain would wear it forever, and his later brothers would know to leave him alone.

Cain went out and built a city, a city built in defiance of God, a counterfeit Garden, a counterfeit Jerusalem. He built it, so to speak, on the blood of his brother, not on the blood of God's appointed substitute. It was the first city of man, but not the last. Later, Rome was built on the blood of Remus, which was shed by Romulus in his rage. The cities and cultures of secular humanism have been built on brothers' blood ever since. The rivers of blood spilled by Adolf Hitler, Fidel Castro, and Idi Amin, and the oceans of blood poured out by Josef Stalin and Margaret Sanger, are but the most recent examples.

A city built on brother's blood cannot last. It has no community, only fear and conflict: Who will be the next to die? It is built on force, not grace. It is imposed by fear, not grown by love. There is no true community in the city of man, only radical individualism—every man for himself. As time went along, the violence in Cain's city increased until finally it came to be celebrated in song (Gen. 4:23–24).

There was another song being sung, however.

Worship Reestablished

After Abel's death, Adam and Eve had another son, Seth. "And to Seth, to him also a son was born; and he called his name Enosh ['Lowly Man']. Then they [plural] began to call upon the Name, Yahweh" (Gen. 4:26).

There was true community among God's people. They joined their hearts weekly and at festival times to sing God's psalms. In their worship they confessed their beast-like sins and gave thanks to God for life and redemption. Thus, they were restored to the basic principle of true dominion—thanksgiving—and as they worked with the world, they worked to restore and transform it.

We know little about the true and godly heroes of that early time. Their spirits must have been vexed by the horrors they saw all around them in the cities of Cain, yet they continued to be faithful.

One of those heroes, however, we do know a little about. His name was Enoch. He spoke out against the evils of his time, and we have his message encapsulated for us in the epistle of Jude. Writing under divine inspiration, Jude tells us that "Enoch, the seventh from Adam, prophesied, saying 'Behold, the Lord came with His holy myriads, to execute judgment upon all, and to convict all the *ungodly* of their *ungodly* deeds that they have done in an *ungodly* way, and of all the harsh things that *ungodly* sinners have spoken against Him'" (Jude 14–15).

Enoch did not mince words with the wicked. Was his life threatened? I imagine so. Was he driven from city to city? Unquestionably. Yet he kept on calling men to repent, to return to the true worship of God. "Your civilization cannot last, unless you build it on faith, on thanksgiving," he warned. "God will destroy it, unless you destroy yourselves first." Enoch did not seek first his own security but the glory of God, and God was pleased with Him. Enoch was taken by God to Himself without seeing death (Gen. 5:21–24).

Jude, in verse 16, tells us about thankless men. He tells us that the people Enoch called to repent were grumblers. One cannot be both a grumbler and a grateful man. They were faultfinders. One cannot go around finding fault with others if one has a heart of thankfulness to God. They followed their own lusts; the thankful man is trained to follow God's desires. They were arrogant in speech; the thankful man learns humility before the throne of God. Finally, they flattered people for the sake of advantage, something the thankful man, secure in God's promises, does not need to do.

True dominion comes from a thankful spirit and hard work according to God's pattern. In the era before the flood, God determined to let evil have its way, so that the righteous did not gain dominion. All the same, they proclaimed the only principles by which any lasting kingdom can come.

Worship and Dominion

The worship that God established through Seth and his descendants, especially Enoch, was designed to restore men to dominion. Men would have to hear the call of the gospel and repent of their ungodliness. Then they would be welcome at the altar. At the altar they would find a pattern of worship that would focus their minds on the true principles of life and labor. It is easiest for us to see this if we look at the structure of worship Jesus set up for us in the New Covenant, but we must remember that the same basic structure was found among God's people of old.

In practical terms, Jesus set at the center of His Kingdom a rite designed to restructure our thinking and reset the course of our living. He did this by establishing the twofold (first bread and then wine) ritual of the Lord's Supper, a ritual that restores us to the holy sixfold action.

1. Jesus took bread and afterwards took the cup of wine.
2. Jesus gave thanks for the bread and later for the wine.
3. Jesus restructured the bread by (a) breaking it and (b) renaming it His body. He restructured wine by renaming it His blood.
4. Jesus distributed it to all present.
5. They all tasted of it. "O taste and see that the Lord is good" (Ps. 34:8). All but one evaluated it as good. Judas evaluated it as bad—assuming for the sake of argument that Judas was still present when the Lord's Supper was instituted.
6. After Judas left, the godly disciples remained with Jesus, enjoying His fellowship and His teaching for a time (Jn. 14–17).

The performance of this weekly rite in worship lies at the heart of true Christian piety. It is seen in both major sections of the traditional worship service. Its performance in Holy Communion (the Lord's Supper or Eucharist) is obvious, but it is also performed in the preaching part of the service. In virtually every kind of church, regardless how "non liturgical" it may seek to be, during the time of proclamation the Word is first read, then thanks is offered, and then the Word is preached. The rite as applied to proclamation is:

1. The reader lays hold of the Word, reading a portion or portions of it without comment.
2. Thanks is offered for the Word and a request is made that the Spirit bless the exposition of it.
3. The Word is broken down and restructured in the preaching of it, and in that preaching . . .
4. The Word is distributed to the people listening.
5. The people evaluate what they hear. By that I do not mean to imply that the people are obligated to pass some kind of professional judgment on the sermon, but that they inevitably will evaluate what they hear.
6. Assuming they find it good and profitable, the people will take the message and inspiration and integrate it into their lives, finding enjoyment therein.

Not only is the performance of the rite in worship the heart of liturgical piety, but it also restores us to true practical piety. Jesus gives us the pattern we are to follow in all of life. Because of His work we can, through Him, lay hold on the fallen creation, no matter how perverse it has become, giving thanks for it, and going to work on it, restoring and transforming it progressively to the glory of God.

By transfiguring (a mystery) bread into His body, Jesus provides a model for the nature of His entire kingdom. The church is also called Christ's body, meaning that the action of bringing men into the church is parallel to the transfiguration of bread into Christ's flesh. Men are broken, cut in half by the covenant Word (Heb. 4:12), and restructured into the body of Christ.[1] Eve (the Bride of Christ) is cut off from her one flesh relationship with Adam and restructured into one-flesh (by the Spirit) with the New Adam. The fallen first creation, whether bread or people, is transfigured by death and resurrection into union with Christ. Indeed, since all things are in Christ, not only men but also the entire cosmos are progressively transformed by being restructured (repositioned) into the "cosmic body" of Christ.[2]

Thus, the structure of liturgical piety and practical piety is the same: the sixfold action. The redemptive key to both is thanksgiving in Christ. Liturgical piety serves practical piety by setting the basic pattern in the Lord's Supper, which men then follow as they go out to transform the world.

The distinction between the true worshiper and the renegade thus lies at the point of *thanksgiving*. It is not possible to take hold of the world with the intention of sinning and still give thanks to God for it. A man cannot enter a store, lay hold on goods with the intention to pocket and steal them, and then give thanks to God.

"Eucharist" means "thanksgiving," and the Eucharistic liturgy that grew up rapidly and organically around the basic sixfold rite of the Supper stressed thanksgiving. This is still seen

---

[1] Covenant-making in the Bible always entails the act of dividing and restructuring. Thus, Eve was divided from Adam and then rejoined to him in the one-flesh relationship. Similarly, when covenant was made with Abraham, the animals were divided in half (Gen. 15).

[2] As Paul writes, "He delivered us from the domain of darkness, and *transferred* us to the kingdom of His beloved Son." By the act of creation, "in Him all things hold together," and as a result of His work of redemption, "all things" are reconciled to God, "whether things on earth or things in heaven." All are brought into the "cosmic body politic" of Christ (Col. 1:13–23; see also Rom. 8:19–22).

in liturgical churches today. The following, or something like it, is found in the worship of all the historic churches that have preserved the early Church's liturgical forms.[3]

In the preface the pastor, after the *sursum corda* ("lift up your hearts," an ascent into heaven for worship), says, "Let us give thanks unto the Lord our God," to which the people reply, "It is fitting and right to do so."

Continuing, the minister prays, "It is truly fitting, right, and healthy that we should at *all* times and in *all* places give thanks unto You," affirming that thanksgiving must characterize all that we do, not just Sunday worship. "Therefore, with angels and archangels, and all the company of heaven, we laud and magnify Your glorious name," he says, whereupon follows the *sanctus,* ascribing praise to God for His holiness.

This *sanctus* hymn is very important. The text is "Holy, holy, holy, Yahweh, God of Armies, heaven and earth are full of the majesty of Your glory." It comes from Isaiah 6:3 and Revelation 4:8, and it is the song sung by the angelic guardians of God's throne. Remember, Adam was originally commissioned to be the guard. He failed and was replaced by the cherubim. Now, in Christ, Christians are restored to the dignity of throne guardians. The historic liturgy reminds us of this incredible privilege.

The eucharistic prayer that follows includes thanksgiving as well: "Remembering therefore His salutary precept, His life-giving suffering and death, His glorious resurrection and ascension, and the promise of His coming again, we give thanks to You, Almighty God, not as we ought but as we are able."

---

[3] For a history of these prayers and their development, see Louis Bouyer, *Eucharist: Theology and Spirituality of the Eucharistic Prayer,* trans. by C. U. Quinn (Notre Dame: University of Notre Dame Press, [1966] 1968).

After the Lord's Supper, the pastor exhorts the congregation, "O give thanks to the Lord, for He is good," to which the people reply, "And His mercy endures forever." There follows another prayer of thanksgiving: "We give thanks to You, Almighty God, that You have refreshed us with this salutary gift." The service closes with the *benedicamus*. The officiant says "Bless we the Lord!" and the congregation shouts "Thanks be to God!"

In this way, worship keys the believer into the proper frame of mind for all of life. Since men continually and unceasingly engage in acts of restructuring, distributing, and evaluating, it is impossible to sort out every action in life and engage in a particular act of thanksgiving at the appropriate spot in the sequence. We do not ordinarily stop to give thanks, for instance, when we get a glass from the cabinet, to return to the example used in chapter one. All the same, there are certain specific times in the day when, according to the consensus of Christian wisdom of all ages, it is appropriate to stop and give thanks. The most obvious of these is mealtimes—after all, it was in connection with a meal that Adam and Eve refused to give thanks and fell into sin. After the food has been set on the table (so that we visually "take hold" of it), we offer thanks and then get to work eating it (restructuring, appreciating, etc.). Similarly, the first thing in the morning, before we lay hold on the day's chores and events, we should give thanks. Public meetings used to begin with prayer, before everyone got down to work. In all these ways the simple sixfold rite is applied constantly in daily life, and so the kingdom comes.

The stress on thanksgiving in liturgical piety is thus the key to practical or laborial piety. In the early Church all life was thus worship, either the special worship of the rite of covenant renewal with God or the general worship of thanksgiving in all of life (1 Thes. 5:18). This worship-centered piety was characteristic of the earliest church, and it must become ours today.

Conclusion

Adam's worship of God had thanksgiving at its center. Because of sin, men must confess sin before they can give thanks. God sends His people out to convict the world of sin through the proclamation of His message, His good news. When men repent, they lay their hands on God's Appointed Sacrifice (Jesus Christ) and confess that they deserve to die but that Jesus has taken their sins. Then they enter into God's palace and give Him thanks, their hearts and minds being retrained to the proper attitude: gratitude. Only such men can build a lasting civilization, built upon the Rock, so that when the floods come, they will be secure.

3   FAITH AND REST
The Story of Noah

Noah was born into a world filled with violence and anarchy. After Cain murdered Abel, the wickedness and savagery of his line increased generation by generation, until the seventh generation. Here we come to Lamech, whose brutality is celebrated in poetry (Gen. 4:23–24).

This was bad enough in itself, but it appears further that in this period there was no God-given institutional restraint on violence. When Cain killed Abel, instead of putting Cain to death as the law of God would later require, God preserved his life. It is only after the flood that we read anything about capital punishment and the institution of godly civil government to restrain men (Gen. 9:5–6). Violence was virtually unchecked before the flood. God apparently wanted to let man have his own way in order to show the effects of maturing sin.

The violence and corruption in Cainite society was bad enough. Sadly, however, the line of godly Seth was seduced by that of Cain. We read in Genesis 6 that "when men began to multiply on the face of the land, and daughters were born to them, that the sons of God saw that the daughters of men were good; and they took wives for themselves, whomever they chose" (vv. 1–2).

Numerous interpretations have been suggested for these verses. Some have felt that the "sons of God" were fallen angels, though how angels could intermarry with women has never been explained. Nor does this interpretation seem to offer anything of relevance to the historical situation described in Genesis.

In the context of Genesis we need an explanation for what happened to the godly line of Seth and why no one but Noah was preserved. We need an explanation of the "fall" of the Sethites. If the "sons of God" are Sethites, as most classical conservative commentators believe, then we have that explanation. Just as Eve *saw* that the forbidden fruit was *good* (Gen. 3:6), so here the Sethites *saw* that the forbidden daughters of Cain were *good*. They willfully intermarried with them, putting their own desires before holiness. As a result the Sethites were also corrupted, and violence became well nigh universal.[1]

Violence

It is useful to stop and reflect on violence, because (sadly) it is part of human nature since the Fall. There are six aspects of violence that we can call attention to.

First, *the murder of God*. Sinful man hates God and would like to kill Him. Man hates God and wants to destroy everything that reminds him of God. God is life, so man hates life and loves death. As the proverb says, all those who hate God "love death" (Prov. 8:35–36). Sinful men hate Christians since they most closely resemble God. This is why they killed Jesus and the prophets. Also, each sinful man hates himself since he is made in the image of God. Additionally, sinful men hate each other since all are made in God's image. Finally, sinful men hate the creation since the creation reflects the glory of God. Thus, violence and killing are innate to sinful man.

Second, *sinful men want to play god*. They want to impose and legislate their fantasies onto the world. When other people resist his totalitarian designs, the sinner resorts to violence to get his way. The sinner wants absolute dominion (sovereignty) over everything. To the extent that God crosses his plans, he is

---

[1] We can probably date the time of the fall of the Sethites into the sin of intermarriage as the time of Enoch. Jude quotes Enoch against Christians who have fallen away. This indicates that Enoch's words against ungodliness were addressed first and foremost to the Sethites, and only secondarily to the Cainites.

frustrated. The saint learns to relax in God's providences, but the rebel seeks to impose his will on circumstances apart from God's will.

Third, *vengeance.* Vengeance is basic to a world in sin. Sin must be dealt with; wrongs must be avenged. God alone is Avenger, though He carefully delegates this work in some measure to civil magistrates (Rom. 12:19; 13:4). Blood vengeance is related to sacrifice, for if a man will not own his sin and take Christ as his Sacrifice, he will make someone else the scapegoat and sacrifice him, as Cain did Abel. Thus, sinful men will always exercise violence against those they choose to blame for their misfortunes.

Fourth, *sado-masochism.* Guilt is basic to sinful man. If a man will not have Christ as his atonement, he will either try to pay for his guilt himself (masochism) or try to make someone else pay for it (sadism). Since a guilty man wants everyone to share his guilt, and is deeply offended if people claim to be innocent, his masochism and sadism go together like two sides of a coin.[2]

Fifth, *dominion.* Man was created to exercise dominion. The urge to rule and take dominion is present in every man to some degree. Sinful man, however, being innately irresponsible, does not want to work for dominion. Instead he tries to get dominion through violence: war (conquest) and enslavement.

Sixth, *revolution.* God rules through authority structures. Hatred of authority stems from hatred of God. Thus, sinful man has a natural tendency to resent authority and exercise violence against it, whether the authorities are good, bad, or relatively indifferent.

Only the preaching of the gospel can cure violence. God established civil government to restrain violence, to hold it in check, but only regeneration can transform the heart of a man and lead to true and peaceful living.

---

[2] For a good series of essays on this theme, see Rousas J. Rushdoony, *Politics of Guilt and Pity* (Phillipsburg: Craig Press, 1970).

The Witness of Noah

In the face of all this violence, the call to repentance was sounded. Lamech, the prophet of violence, the seventh from Adam in Cain's line, was matched by Enoch, the prophet of God, who was seventh from Adam in Seth's line. Noah followed in Enoch's footsteps, for we read in 2 Peter 2:5 that God "did not spare the ancient world, but preserved Noah, *a preacher of righteousness,* with seven others, when He brought a flood upon the world of the ungodly."

Not only did Noah preach with his lips, he also engaged in a 120-year long project that was a visual witness against the ungodly: building the Ark.[3] "By faith Noah, being warned about things not yet seen, in reverence prepared an ark for the salvation of his household, by which he condemned the world" (Heb. 11:7). Building the Ark was a sign that the flood was coming. As the wicked saw it being erected day by day, they saw a visible witness, a visible proclamation of the truth of coming judgment. They may have ridiculed it. They may have torched the project over and over again—120 years is a long time to build a ship unmolested. They may have harassed Noah in many ways, but their hearts told them that God is God and that He will not abide evil forever.

In this way Noah strove against wickedness as his fathers had. Yet, when Noah was born, his godly father Lamech (a new and different Lamech) prophesied, "This one will comfort us from our work and from the toil of our hands arising from the ground, which Yahweh has cursed" (Gen. 5:29). Lamech named his son "Noah," meaning "Rest."

Lamech's prophecy is couched in symbolic language. God had told Adam that the ground would henceforth be cursed

---

[3] It seems that Noah took 120 years to build the Ark. Compare 1 Peter 3:20 and Genesis 6:3.

"with reference to you.[4] In toil you will eat of it all the days of your life. Both thorns and thistles it will grow for you; and you will eat the plant of the field; by the sweat of your nostrils you will eat bread until you return to the ground, because from it you were taken; for you are dust, and to dust you will return" (Gen. 3:17–19). It is literally true that the ground gives forth thorns and weeds, and the labor of man is rendered difficult as a result of God's curse mediated through the ground.

This dimension of the curse does not exhaust its meaning, however. Remember that man himself is made of the ground. We are told this in Genesis 2:7 and again in Genesis 3:19, in the very context of the curse. Under the influence of the Spirit of God, the ground "gave birth" to man. The first man was made a "tree," but now, after the Fall, the ground would bring up "thorns." As a result, in the Bible good trees are symbols for righteous men, while thorns and brambles are symbols for violent and ungodly men. We see this in Psalm 1, Judges 9, and Matthew 7:17–19. Man is made of the ground, so the offspring of men are either trees or thorns. Such symbolism may be unfamiliar to twentieth-century Christians, but it was common in the ancient world.

In terms of this symbolism we can understand why Genesis 4 is written as it is. We aren't shown Adam laboring to pull up weeds from his field by the sweat of his brow, which is what we might expect to be shown as the fulfillment of the curse. Rather, we see a thorn (Cain) murder a tree (Abel).

Indeed, understanding this symbolism helps us see the one way God did restrain evil in the centuries before the flood. God told Cain, "When you cultivate the ground, it will no longer yield its strength to you" (Gen. 4:12). While this was no doubt literally true, the intensified curse mediated through the ground

---

[4] The ground, which after all did not sin against God, was not directly cursed. Rather, the meaning is that the good, God-honoring soil will mediate God's judgments to man. The soil is on God's side and thus stands against sinners.

carried with it an implication that Cain's line would be sickly and weak because of sin. Why was Cain's line strong, then? How were they able to dominate the world—so much so that God determined to destroy it? By intermarrying with the mighty line of Seth! The Bible is teaching us that the wicked do not have strength in themselves. Only when the godly foolishly lend their strength to the wicked are the wicked able to prosper.[5]

Now we are in a better position to understand the prophecy of the godly Lamech. He saw that Noah (Rest) would give comfort from the curse mediated through the ground, not in the sense that the literal curse of thorns would be lifted (for it wasn't), but in the sense that the curse of the overwhelming presence of wicked and violent men would be dealt with. The righteous would receive rest from the "toil of our hands," the toil of prophesying against and resisting the wicked.

And so Noah labored in the hope of rest. As he toiled to build the Ark, so he toiled to warn men—year after year, and without any success except with his sons and their families. Yet he believed God, and He believed the God-given prophecy concerning his name. God would give rest in due time—through the flood.

Resting Faith

And so it came to pass. The Flood washed away the wicked world, and Noah rested in a new creation. No longer did he need to strive against the ungodly "thorns." Three dimensions of this resting faith stand out: Worship, relaxation and enthronement.

---

[5] The great violence that has so often characterized "Western Civilization" is due precisely to the marriage of Christian faith with Greco-Roman philosophy and social thinking.

Worship

The first thing Noah did after leaving the Ark was to worship God. "Then Noah built an altar to Yahweh, and took of every clean animal and of every clean bird and offered ascension offerings[6] on the altar" (Gen. 8:20). Thus he confessed that he, too, was a sinner, and that he, too, deserved to die in the flood. But Noah also confessed that his sins were covered in the sacrifice and that he had survived the flood not because of his righteousness, but because of the righteousness of the Sacrifice to come. The slaughter of these animals pointed to that future Sacrifice.

This is the only time in Scripture that "every clean beast and bird" is sacrificed at once. It symbolized a judgment on the whole animal kingdom that Adam had named and then polluted. It symbolized that the whole creation had been killed and resurrected.[7] It made possible a new creation—a new Garden with "new animals" to name. It was a passage from wrath to grace. It was Noah's pledge that, if he had anything to do with it, the new world would be different from the old.

God responded to Noah's worship with a pledge that the new world would indeed be better. There would never again be a Flood. In the future, God would act in man's youth to prevent sin from maturing to the point of universal destruction. We see this promise by comparing Genesis 8:21 with 6:5. Genesis 6:5 reads that "every intent of the thoughts of [man's] heart was only evil continually." Genesis 8:21 says virtually the same thing but with one change: "The intent of man's heart is evil *from his*

---

[6] "Burnt offering" is literally "ascension offering."

[7] That is, killed in the flood, and then again in the killing of the sacrifices. Placing the sacrificed animals into the fire (symbol of God's presence) is a symbol of resurrection, and their going up in smoke is a symbol of ascension. The act of sacrifice includes the promise of resurrection.

youth. " This implies that God will intervene in man's youth to cut off sin and bring in righteousness. We shall see exactly this in our next chapter.

Rest and Relaxation

The second dimension of resting faith that we can see is personal rest and relaxation. "Then Noah began to be a farmer and planted a vineyard" (Gen. 9:20). This is a new Garden of Eden presided over by Noah, the image of God. "And he drank of the wine and became drunk, and uncovered himself inside his tent" (Gen. 9:21). Because this sentence is so often misunderstood, we need to take a couple of paragraphs to deal with it.

In the Bible, wine is for joy (Judg. 9:13; Ps. 104:15). It is a picture of future blessings, when the curse mediated through the ground (thorns, brambles) is overcome and the vine and fig tree flourish. It thus has a close tie to the sabbath, to the time when a man's work is finished and he can relax in the presence of God. As a sign that he had completed the task set before him for the moment, Abram was given wine by Melchizedek (Gen. 14:18). Similarly, at the annual Feast of Clouds (Booths; Tabernacles), Israel was encouraged to drink wine and "strong drink" (beer) and make merry in the presence of God (Deut. 14:26). Indeed, it is wine as well as bread that is the very sign of the New Covenant![8]

So after the flood, in sabbath rest, Noah planted a vineyard, and drank of the wine. He got "drunk," but all this means is that he became relaxed and went to sleep. Nothing in the least indicates that Noah was a habitual drunkard, since such a lifestyle is condemned in the Bible. Noah uncovered himself

---

[8] Pastorally speaking, some people have difficulty with alcohol, and choose not to drink it. Our purpose here is not to deal with that legitimate concern, but to discuss the meaning of the biblical message.

in the privacy of his tent, laying aside the robe of his office and duties. It was a time for sabbath relaxation. (Sadly, there was a serpent in his garden, Ham, but we shall discuss him in our next chapter.)

In the Lord's Supper, God wants Christians to relax and drink wine in His presence. Such rest comes at the end of our duties, not during them of course, but it is the promise of rest and joy for every Christian toiler.

Enthronement

Until this time God had never committed to any man the right to exercise rule and government. Adam had failed in his *warrior* task of guarding the garden and had never been given a robe of glory or a throne of judgment. Now, however, such responsibilities were delegated to man. God said to Noah, "And surely I will require your lifeblood; from every beast will I require it. And from the hand of every man, from the hand of every man's brother I will require the life of man" (Gen. 9:5). In other words, if brother kills brother in the future, as Cain slew Abel, human courts are to put that man to death. "Whoever sheds man's blood, by man his blood shall be shed, for in the image of God He made man" (Gen. 9:6).

When God gives to Christians the right to rule they must not shrink from the hard task of passing judgments. Noah lived for six hundred years before the flood. Though he never met his great-grandfather Enoch, he was trained in righteousness by his grandfather Methuselah and his father Lamech. He prophesied against wickedness his whole life, especially in the last 120 years before the flood. Now God gave him rest and made him a ruler, a captain of a new creation, a new and better Adam: Noah was no longer only "a little lower than God" but was "crowned with glory and honor" (Ps. 8:5). Noah had fought Satan for six hundred years and earned the robe of office that

Adam had forfeited. He was soon forced to use his office and authority against a serpent in his own household, his son Ham.[9]

Conclusion

The story of Noah is a comfort for Christians today. Faced with ungodliness on every side, we do not have rule or dominion. We live in a time of prophecy and Ark-building, warning the wicked and building the Church. In time, however, God will destroy the wicked, either through plague or conversion, and give rule to His people. The wine we drink in Holy Communion and the robes our church officers wear are our pledge that this is so. Like Noah, we must never shrink from our duty.

---

[9] For a much fuller discussion of the sabbath and enthronement, see chapter three of my book, *Sabbath-Breaking and the Death Penalty: A Theological Investigation* (Tyler:Geneva Ministries, 1986; photocopy available from Biblical Horizons, Box 1096, Niceville, FL, 32588).

4 FAITH AND REBELLION
The Stories of Ham and Nimrod

We turn now to two examples demonstrating false humanistic faith and how God acted to frustrate it. God will not permit the unrighteous to exercise long-term authority, and the stories of Ham's rebellion and the Tower of Babel demonstrate this, to the encouragement of the saints.

The Judgment of Ham

In order for us to understand the sin of Ham we need to realize that the Bible presents him as a *righteous* man before the flood. Scholars have debated whether the sons of Noah were saved only because of their union with Noah or because of their own faith. It seems clear that the latter is the case. The point of the passage is to teach that the Lord requites every man according to his deeds: the righteous man according to his faithfulness and the wicked man according to his faithlessness. Also, we are told that Noah was a wholly righteous man (Gen. 6:9), and such righteousness would have to include training his sons to walk in the fear of God.[1] Thus, Ham was a righteous man before the flood, and when he sinned, he lapsed from grace.[2]

We saw in the last chapter that Noah, having come to a time of sabbath rest, "drank of the wine [of his New-Garden vineyard] and became drunk, and uncovered himself inside his tent" (Gen. 9:21). Noah's robe was a sign of his office and

---

[1] On this point see Umberto Cassuto, *A Commentary on the Book of Genesis, Part II: From Noah to Abraham,* trans. Israel Abrahams (Jerusalem: Magnes Press, [1949] 1964), pp. 50–51. Cassuto also calls attention to Ezekiel 14:14–20 in this regard, to prove that Noah could not have saved his own sons had they not been faithful men.

[2] Whether Ham was elect or not, and whether he was *truly regenerate* or not, is God's concern, not ours. The saints are called to persevere in faithful righteousness, and Ham did not do so. Or at least he lapsed into sin at one important point in his life. Perhaps he repented and was delivered. We are not told.

authority[3] In the privacy of his tent, he laid it aside. There was no sin in this; after all, he was still covered by the "garment" of the tent itself.

The sin of Ham is recorded in Genesis 9:22: "And Ham, the father of Canaan, saw the nakedness of his father, and told his two brothers outside." Down through the ages certain commentators have speculated on the sin of Ham. Does this verse imply a homosexual attack? Does it imply that Ham castrated Noah? The text provides no hint of such notions. Actually, the sin consisted of something more fundamental: rebellion against authority. This can be seen from the actions of Shem and Japheth. What they did was designed to undo what Ham had done, and all they did was refuse to look upon their father's nakedness while upholding his office by robing him: "But Shem and Japheth took *the* garment[4] and laid it upon both their shoulders and walked backward and covered the nakedness of their father; and their faces were turned backward, so that they did not see their father's nakedness" (Gen. 9:23). The curse pronounced by Noah is phrased in terms of authority and submission. The sin here is rebellion, not some kind of sexual attack.

We have seen that one of the changes after the flood is that man is given the authority to exercise capital punishment against murderers. In other words, human authority was established at that time. God delegated certain judicial responsibilities to man by appointing or allowing certain men to rule over others. The earlier rebellion of Adam had been against God's authority and rule. Now that men have been given rule we can anticipate a rebellion against this human authority. That is exactly what happened.

---

[3] For more on the robe, see chapter 10.

[4] English translations obscure the Hebrew by rendering "a garment." It is doubtless Noah's special robe of authority that is in view. "Shem and Japheth acted to preserve the honor of their father by covering him with *the* garment (Gen. 9:23). The impression is that Ham completed the nakedness by bringing the garment out to his brothers." Allen P. Ross, "The Curse of Canaan," *Bibliotheca Sacra* 137 (1980):231.

Ham "saw the nakedness of his father" (Gen. 9:22). How could he? His father was inside a tent—not just some little tee-pee but a real, house-sized tent. Ham had to *invade* Noah's privacy without permission. Ham was *seeking to uncover a fault* in his superior so that he could tear down his authority.

Then Ham "told his two brothers outside" (Gen. 9:22). Ham was not going to try to take down Noah by himself. No, he tried to enlist his brothers in the project, perhaps arguing: "Father has laid aside his robe of office. We can take it and make ourselves rulers." Back in the garden, Satan had said to Adam and Eve, "You can make yourselves gods by taking the forbidden fruit." Satan now said to the heart of Ham, who repeated it to his brothers, "You can make yourselves kings by stealing the robe of office."

Shem and Japheth refused to join Ham's conspiracy. To dramatize their support for their father they "took the garment and laid it upon both their shoulders and walked backward and covered the nakedness of their father" (Gen. 9:23). They did not have to do this. Noah was still covered by the tent itself. Nor did they have to go to the trouble of putting the garment on both their shoulders and walking backward. They did this for a symbolic reason. The shoulders are associated with pillars of support, and by putting the garment on their shoulders (instead of carrying it in their hands), they were symbolically upholding Noah's office.[5] Since nakedness is associated with shame in fallen men (Gen. 2:25; 3:7), they refused to look at their father. They refused to shame or embarrass him in any way.

Respect for established order and authority is one of the cardinal keys to dominion. We find in the fifth commandment: "Honor your father and your mother, that your days may be

---

[5] Symbolically, it took two of them to hold up Noah's "heavy" robe. (In Hebrew, "glorious" and "heavy" are the same word.) In other words, they confessed that individually they were not yet ready for such a burden. On shoulders and pillars, see Meredith G. Kline, *Images of the Spirit* (Grand Rapids: Baker, 1980), pp. 44–45.

long in the land that Yahweh your God gives you." Accordingly, Noah blessed Shem and Japheth with enlargement of dominion.

The reverse is also true. Rebellion and revolution against established order and authority is the quickest road to slavery. "When Noah awoke from his wine, he knew what his youngest son had done to him. So he said, 'Cursed be Canaan; a slave of slaves shall he be to his brothers'" (Gen. 9:24–25). Just as Noah's son had rebelled against him, so Ham's son would rebel against him. Like father, like son. Ham had three other sons, but it seems Noah discerned the tendency to rebellion in Canaan, and so he pronounced the curse upon that son. Rebellion leads to slavery, and as the generations go by the slavery worsens. The wars of Genesis 14 show that the Canaanites were already dominated by Japhethites and Shemites by the time of Abram and were unable to shake off their yoke. As the centuries went by, the Canaanites' enslavement to sin became progressively worse until finally God destroyed them.

We are told explicitly that Noah "knew what his *youngest* son had done to him" (Gen. 9:24). This ties in with the statement of Genesis 8:21 that "the intent of man's heart is evil *from his youth.*" Here we see that God acts to prevent such youthful evil from maturing to full age. Ham's rebellion is blocked. God intervenes, through Noah, to spare His people from the kind of horrors that went on before the flood. The fall of Adam, repeated in the fall of Ham, will not be permitted to run its full course again. This is a promise to the righteous that over the long haul it will be the godly who inherit the earth, not the wicked.

The Judgment of Nimrod

The sin of Adam, who stole fruit, was followed by the sin of Cain, who built a city. Similarly, the sin of Ham, who sought to steal a robe, was followed by the sin of Nimrod, who sought to build a city. Nimrod did not succeed any more than did

Ham, and thus the comfort of God's judgment against the wicked is reiterated.

Nimrod was Ham's grandson, though by Cush rather than Canaan. Perhaps the Canaanites were already too slavish to do the kinds of "mighty" works Nimrod did. Nimrod founded two cities that grew into two of the mightiest empires of the ancient world: Babylon and Nineveh (Assyria). Genesis 10:8–12 tells us that he built Babylon first and then moved to Assyria. The story of the Tower of Babel explains his move.

As we begin the story of the Tower of Babel we read, "Now the whole earth used the same language and the same words" (Gen. 11:1). This common translation does not bring out the meaning of the Hebrew, for the word translated *language* in this verse actually means *lip*. The phrase "same words" refers to language, but the phrase "same lip"—literally "one lip"—refers to religion.[6]

Now the idea of speaking one language or another is not absolutely excluded from this word *lip* (see Is. 19:18), but in the context of Genesis 11, there is clearly a difference between the "one lip [confession, ideology]" and the "one words [vocabulary]" of verse one. What happened at the Tower of Babel was not first and foremost a division of languages, but rather a division of religious belief, as we shall see more fully below.

"And it came to pass, as they journeyed east, that they found a plain in the land of Shinar, and they dwelt there" (Gen. 11:2). Just as Cain moved away from God by moving east (Gen. 4:6), so this "eastward" movement indicates movement away from God. But who was moving eastward? Nimrod? No. In Genesis 10:25–30 we read, within the immediate context of the story of the Tower of Babel, that it was certain Hebrews, descendants of Shem, who were moving eastward.

[6] Zephaniah 3:9; Psalm 81:5; Job 27:4; 33:3; Psalms 12:2–4; 16:4; 40:9; 45:2; 51:15; Isaiah 6:5; 6:7; Malachi 2:6–7.

From this fact we see that the Tower of Babel was not only a repeat of the sin of Cain in building a false city, but also a repeat of the intermarriage of the sons of God with the daughters of men. Renegade Hebrews joined with Nimrod in building the false tower and the false city. The false tower was the citadel, the false worship center that was to reach up to the heavens. Associated with the renegade Hebrews' tower was the false "lip" or religion of these people. The false city was the culture that was being built around the tower. Associated with Nimrod's city was the language of these people.

"And they said to one another, 'Come, let us make bricks and burn them thoroughly.' And they used brick for stone, and they used tar for mortar. And they said, 'Come, let us build for ourselves a city, and a tower whose top is in the heavens; and let us make for ourselves a name; lest we be scattered abroad over the face of the whole earth'" (Gen. 11:3–4). God had told both Adam and Noah (Gen. 9:1) to spread out and fill the earth. In rebellion, Nimrod and his cohorts did not want to take dominion. They did not want to build the city of God nor gather around His tower of true worship, growing slowly and gradually by faith. Rather, like Cain before them, they wanted an instant city, gathered around false religion, built on power and might.

Cain had built his city on the human sacrifice of his brother (Gen. 4). We are told that Nimrod built his tower of bricks. When we remember that man was made of soil (Gen. 2:7), and that God's House is made of people, "living stones" (1 Pet. 2:4–8), we can see a double meaning in what we read here in Genesis 11. Nimrod's tower of bricks cemented by asphalt served to signify his *unified society of men;* they were all stuck together in one place and not spreading out and taking dominion over the world.

These men knew that their tower—probably a pyramid, a symbolic "holy mountain"—would not physically reach into heaven. It was a religious center that they thought would enable them to storm the gates of heaven and seize the gifts of God's Garden, from which men had been excluded (Gen. 3:24). This is the goal of all pagan works-religion, and it was their goal as well.

We need to notice also that they wanted to make themselves a name. They did not want to be given a name by God or to wear His name. They wanted to make a name for themselves, to glorify themselves. This is analogous to Adam seizing the fruit and Ham seizing the robe.

Reading on: "And Yahweh came down to see the city and the tower that the sons of the man [Adam] had built. And Yahweh said, 'Behold, they are one people, and they all have one lip [ideology]. And this is what they began to do, and now nothing that they propose to do will be impossible for them. Come, let us go down and there confuse their lip, that they may not understand one another's lip'" (Gen. 11:5–7).[7]

It is surprising to hear God say that, because the people are unified, "nothing that they propose to do will be impossible for them." God can always stop men from doing anything, but the language used here points to the fact that in terms of the economy God has established in the world, there is strength in unity. God does not want the wicked to rule the world, so He moves to destroy their unity.

It is important to see that it was not a simple unity of language that gave these men power. Rather, they all *thought* the same way. They had a common "lip," a common ideology, a common religious faith. Without this anti-God unity they could not have cooperated. In order to shatter this unity, God

---

[7] There is a lot of humor in the Bible. The author here pokes fun at the Tower of Babel. It was going to reach into heaven, but God had to "come down" even to see it! Also, in verse 5, the author calls this bunch of rebels "sons of the man." Like Adam and Eve, they wanted to make themselves gods, yet they were nothing but sons of the man (Adam). These Hebrews had fallen from being "sons of God," His spokesmen, to being mere "sons of the man."

did not simply divide their languages. First and foremost, He shattered their ideologies.

What the story of the Tower of Babel tells us is that there was originally only one pagan, anti-God religion in the world. At the Tower of Babel, God acted to diversify paganism. All the heathen religions in the world have the same basic ideas, but each is slightly different from the rest. One group worships Thor and his kin, another Zeus and his family, another Jupiter and his cohorts. One nation favors Baal, another Chemosh, another Molech, and another Amon-Ra. One group of revolutionary socialists follows Marx-and-Lenin, another follows Marx-and-Mao, another Marx-and-Castro, and another Marx-and-Ho Chi Minh. Still others follow Adolf Hitler. From the Christian point of view there are not many differences between these pagan religions, but from their own points of view the differences are great. Each pagan nation has its own "gods," and wars are fought over them.

If it seems strange that God Himself would act to create these different manifestations of the one basic pagan religion, we have to remember that according to Romans 1:18–32 God punishes sin by giving people over to it. Idolatry destroys human life, and if men rebel against God, He will give them over to worse and worse forms of idolatry until either they repent or are destroyed. The punishment fits the crime.

According to Genesis 11:1, the people not only had a common ideology (lip), they also had the same language (vocabulary). The passage clearly implies that God also confounded their languages so that they would not understand one another. Not only did their religions come to be in conflict, but they could not understand one another's words either.

Ever since this time sinful human beings have tended to view people who speak other languages as inferior, or even as only talking animals. The word "barbarian" comes from the way other languages sound in our ears: "bar bar," almost like the barking of dogs. European conquerers treated Africans and Asians as barbarians, seldom bothering to learn their very rich and complex languages, despising the inescapable manifestations of the image of God in these cultures.

The Christian knows that God has established Christianity to create a true unity of confession (lip) among all nations and peoples, but this unity will not destroy the diversity of languages. Instead, each nation and language will praise Him in its own tongue (Rev. 7:9). Enlightened Christians seek to recognize and appreciate the beauty of every language God has put into the human race. Good missionaries do not seek to destroy everything in pagan societies, but rather they bring the Bible to such cultures and let the Bible transform them into true cultures.

At Pentecost (Acts 2), God sent out the gospel in all languages. While the Bible is the original and pure form of God's Word in Hebrew, Aramaic, and Greek, the fullness of His revelation will not come until every language comes to express biblical truth in its own unique way. Every language has a particular set of perspectives on the Word of God, and thus every language is fitted to reveal God and praise Him in a special way. Throughout eternity the saints will delight to learn language after language, learning to praise God in new ways, age after age, forever and ever.

The scattering of languages at the Tower of Babel was not by itself a curse. Rather, it was the multiplication of pagan religions that showed God's judgment against the tower builders. The fact that *God will never permit non-Christians to form a world coalition again* is a blessing to Christians. No matter how hard they try, the pagan dream of a secular "united nations" is doomed to failure. It is the true faith that is destined to triumph in history.

Conclusion

The promise of God to His people is that false rebellious faith
will always be broken off in history. The secular humanist
faith—that man can do great things without God—is always
doomed to frustration and failure. God permitted that faith to
run its full course once, before the flood. He will never permit
it again. Rather, He will intervene in man's youth and cut down
the aspirations of sin, either by conversion or by destruction.
In the case of Ham, it was a man, Noah, who pronounced the
judgment. The story of Babel tells us that if Christian men are
unable (or unwilling) to stop the march of such humanism, God
Himself will intervene to do so. This is part of the comfort of
the saints.

5   FAITH AND PATIENCE

The Story of Abraham

In Hebrews 6, we read that true Christians are "imitators of those who through faith and *patience* inherit the promises. For when God made the promise to Abraham, since He could swear by no one greater, He swore by Himself, saying, 'Blessing I will bless you, and multiplying I will multiply you.' And thus, having *patiently* waited, he obtained the promise" (Heb. 6:12–15).

The recipients of the letter to the Hebrews knew that Jesus Christ had conquered Satan and was now enthroned King of the world. They wondered why they did not yet see all things put under His feet (Heb. 2:8). The answer for them was that God had sworn that they would in time inherit the promise (Heb. 6:12–18), and so they should be patient. A preeminent quality of true faith, thus, is a trust in God that He will, in His own time, accomplish His promise (Heb. 11). Just as Jesus was perfected through wisdom-inducing suffering (Heb. 2:10), so Christians must patiently endure suffering until they are ready to be invested with authority and dominion (Heb. 12).

The example set out for consideration is Abraham, but the importance of patience to faith does not begin with Abraham. It begins in the garden.

Adam's Impatience

When God created Adam and set him to guard the Garden of Eden, He told him, "From any tree of the garden you may eat freely, but from the Tree of the Knowledge of Good and Evil you shall not eat from it, for in the day that you eat from it you will surely die" (Gen. 2:16–17). This is familiar enough, and because it is so well known to us we tend to overlook another statement God made about food. After Eve had been created,

God told Adam and Eve that *every* food-bearing tree He had
created was for them to eat: "Then God said, 'Behold, I have
given you every plant yielding seed that is on the face of all the
earth, and every tree in which is the fruit of a tree yielding seed;
it will be food for you'" (Gen. 1:29). (We know that God made
this statement after Eve was created because in Gen. 1:28, the
preceding verse, He was speaking to both of them.)

What does this mean? It means that the prohibition the fruit
of the Tree of the Knowledge of Good and Evil was temporary.
Adam and Eve knew they eventually would be allowed to eat of
it if they were patient. The test before them involved not just
sheer obedience to a command from God but also patience and
hope of reward.

The Bible explains to us that this Tree of the Knowledge of
Good and Evil is associated with enthronement and rule. It has
to do with the privilege of making judicial pronouncements.
In Genesis 1, we repeatedly see God pronouncing things good.
Adam was to understand that he was not yet ready, not yet
mature enough to make his own pronouncements regarding
good and evil. Until that time, he was supposed to accept God's
judgments by faith. He was not to seize the prerogatives of rule.

The kind of knowledge spoken of here is not *moral* knowledge of right and wrong but *judicial knowledge,* the right to pass
judgments under God. The best way to understand this, the
biblical way, is to consider the difference between a child and
an adult. Children know right from wrong; it is written on their
hearts. Yet they are not mature or experienced enough to pass
judgments on situations. Parents tell them what to do, and they
are to obey. The Bible speaks of children as those who "have no
knowledge of good or evil" (Deut. 1:39).

It is adults, and especially rulers, who have this special judicial knowledge. Solomon prayed to be given "an understanding heart to *judge* Your people, to *discern* between *good and evil.*

For who is able to *judge* this weighty people of Yours?" (1 Kgs. 3:9). Although he was already king, Solomon did not presume that he already possessed this judicial knowledge. Rather, he asked for it, and God granted it. The next scene in 1 Kings 3 shows us Solomon exercising this judicial knowledge.[1]

It takes years of training and experience to come to the point of being able to pass good judgments. The book of Hebrews comments on this when it says that "solid food is for the mature, who because of practice have their senses trained to discern good and evil" (Heb. 5:14). This experience Adam did not have. Adam was to refrain from the Tree of Judicial Knowledge until God was ready to give it to him.

The prerogatives of judicial authority are not to be seized. Rather, they are to be bestowed. Looking again at the book of Hebrews, which indirectly comments on Adam's impatience, we read in 5:1 that "every high priest is . . . *appointed.*" Reading further we come to verse 4: "And no one takes the honor to himself, but receives it when he is called by God, even as Aaron was. So also Christ did not glorify Himself so as to become a high priest. . . ." It was after His earthly labors that Jesus was "*designated* by God as a high priest" (v. 10).

With all this in mind we can better understand Adam's sin. He refused to wait for God to give him permission to eat the forbidden fruit. He refused to remain a "child of God" for a time. He refused to wait until he was mature enough to handle the load. Instead, he seized the fruit and set himself up as a judicial authority. God honored his decision, but He gave Adam authority only outside the garden. It would not be until Jesus

---

[1] We can also look at what the wise woman said to David in 2 Samuel 14:17: "For as the angel of God, so is my lord the king to discern good and evil." In other words, man's judicial authority is a copy of God's. And see also 2 Samuel 19:20, 27, 35. Notice also Genesis 31:24, "And God came to Laban the Aramean in a dream of the night and said to him, 'Take heed to yourself that you do not speak to Jacob either good or evil.'" Laban had brought men with him to form a law-court to pass judgment on Jacob, but God told Laban that He, not Laban, was Jacob's judge.

Christ that a man would be permitted back into God's heavenly Garden.

During the Old Testament, God taught the principle of patience through the lives of several heroes. In this book we are concerned with Abraham, Jacob, and Joseph, but we could add David to the list: David had to serve under Saul for years, and though tempted to seize the kingdom for himself (1 Sam 24:4–6), David never did so.

Patience and Land

When God called Abraham, then known as Abram, out of Ur of the Chaldeans, He made several promises to him. We are concerned with three. First, God said, "Go forth from your country, and from your relatives, and from your father's house, to the *land* that I will show you" (Gen. 12:1). The other two promises, a great nation and a great name, will concern us in the next two sections of this chapter.

When Abram arrived in Canaan he walked the length of the land. This exploration expressed his trust in God, that God would some day give him this land. He also built two altars, one at Shechem and the second at Bethel (Gen. 12:6–8). These were central and strategic sites that would continue to be important throughout all later Israelite history. By setting up altars Abram was claiming the land for Yahweh.

It is important for us to reflect on the meaning of these altars. They were not just places where Abram offered his personal worship. They were also worship centers for all the faithful in the area. Abram was an evangelist. This is not immediately obvious from the English translations, but in Genesis 12:5 we should read: "And Abram took Sarai his wife and Lot his nephew, and all their possessions which they had accumulated, and the souls that they had *made* in Haran. . . ." The distinguished Jewish commentator Umberto Cassuto explains that the verb we have translated "made" is not the correct term for acquiring servants. Rather, it indicates evangelization. These people were not purchased but converted.[2]

Cassuto points out that the ancient Rabbinic tradition always maintained that Abram was an evangelist, calling attention also to Genesis 12:8. In this latter verse we read that Abram "called on the Name, Yahweh," but a better translation would be "proclaimed the Name, Yahweh." Cassuto writes: "Besides the altar that Abraham built in honor of the Lord, he made proclamations concerning the religion of the Lord to the inhabitants of the land, and thus he continued in the Chosen Land the work that he had already begun when he was in Haran. In view of this, the local people regarded him as a 'prince of God' (Gen. 23:6)."[3]

In seeking to lay claim to Canaan, Abram did not first engage in a military conquest. Rather, his first action was to establish the worship of the true God and work to change the hearts and minds of the people living there. He knew that all cultural benefits flow from worship. He sought first the kingdom of God, trusting that all other things would be given to him later on (Mt. 6:33).

God put Abram's faith through trials, however. No sooner had he begun to settle in the land than God brought a famine, and Abram had to move to Egypt for a time. There his family was attacked, but God graciously delivered him. In the process God greatly increased his property (Gen. 12:10–20). Once back in the land, Abram resumed his ministry of worship (Gen. 13:4, 18).

Peace was not to last, however. The Canaanites of the land were vassals of Chedorlaomer, and they rebelled.

---

[2] Umberto Cassuto, *A Commentary on the Book of Genesis, Part II: From Noah to Abraham*, trans. Israel Abrahams (Jerusalem: Magnes Press, [1949] 1964), p. 320.

[3] *Ibid.*, p. 332. Cassuto calls attention to Exodus 33:19 and 34:5 as other instances where "called on" clearly means "proclaimed."

Chedorlaomer sent an army to subdue the Canaanites. War raged over the promised land, particularly in the area of Sodom where Abram's nephew Lot lived. Having reconquered his subjects, Chedorlaomer left for home, taking Lot among his captives. At this point, Abram rounded up his fighting men and pursued Chedorlaomer to Dan, way in the north. He defeated Chedorlaomer and chased him many miles further north, out of the promised land altogether.

Yet, Abram did not use his strength to consolidate and rule in Canaan. In fact, he refused to accept any of the spoil offered to him by the king of Sodom. Rather, he insisted that he would receive nothing from the hands of men. He would wait upon God, the Possessor of Heaven and Earth (Gen. 14:19, 22). He who possesses all things would give the land to Abram when He was ready.

Abram was afraid that Chedorlaomer would return, and so God appeared to him and told him not to fear. "I am your shield," said the Lord (Gen. 15:1), implying that he need not fear Chedorlaomer. Reassured by God's comforting presence and promise, Abram asked how his possession of the land would come to pass. Yahweh then told him that he himself would not actually take possession of it. Instead, his descendants would inherit the land, but only after an exile of four hundred years (Gen. 15:13). In this way God honored Abram with a fuller insight into His purposes, and Abram came to understand that it was through his children that he would possess the land.

Patience and Seed

The name "Abram" means "Exalted Father." We don't know if this was the name his parents gave him or if God gave him this name when he was called to leave Ur. At any rate, Abram had to carry this name for years, though he had no children because his wife Sarai ("My Princess") was barren. It must have been hard to bear this name. Strangers would ask, "Well, Exalted Father, how many children do you have?"—and Abram would have to answer, "None." It doubtless led to much snickering. Now, however, God told Abram that he would have a child to inherit him, and through his descendants he would possess the land. (Gen. 15:4)

Satan was able to use this promise of God to get Abram to sin. He introduced a forbidden fruit to Abram, and Abram took it. To understand this, let's think back to the Garden of Eden. There were two special trees there: the Tree of Life and the Tree of Judicial Knowledge. Adam was originally encouraged to eat of the Tree of Life (since God had marked it out, and it was not forbidden), but he was told not to eat of the Tree of Judicial Knowledge. God said Adam would die if he ate the forbidden fruit. Satan directly contradicted God's word, and Adam followed him.

The situation is parallel here. Satan's attack was a bit more subtle this time, however. God had told Abram that a child from his own loins would be his heir. Sarai was barren, but there were two women in Abram's immediate "garden." Just as Eve gave the fruit to Adam, so it was Sarai who suggested to Abram that he go in to her maid, Hagar, and seek to bear a child through her.[4] The idea was that Sarai would "be built from" Hagar (Gen. 16:2); that is, that the child born of the surrogate mother would be adopted immediately by Sarai and be her child. Both Sarai and Abram demonstrated impatience and grasped at a blessing that God had told them they would receive eventually, but not yet. Adam sought to rule by eating a forbidden fruit; Abram sought a son by sleeping with a forbidden woman.

Hagar refused to give her son to Sarai in adoption, and the result was strife. Even so, Abram still had hopes for Ishmael,

[4] Hagar the Egyptian was part of Abram's spoil from his exodus from Egypt (Gen. 12:16). Such spoil must be handled carefully. Later, the Israelites made the Tabernacle from the spoil of Egypt, but only after they had first made the Golden Calf with it.

his son. About the time Ishmael was entering puberty, when
Abram could begin thinking of a marriage for his son—and sub-
sequent heirs—God appeared to him again (Gen. 16:16; 17:1).
God told him that Ishmael was not the promised seed and that
Sarai would bear him the needed son. While this was good news,
it essentially put Abram back at square one.

At this point, God changed his name from Abram to
Abraham—"Father of a Multitude" (Gen. 17). We can imagine that this was again something of a trial for Abraham, since
he was then the father of only one child and later of only two.
Yet he wore his name in faith, confident that God, in His time,
would honor His promise.

God sorely tested Abraham's faith right away. After the destruction of Sodom and Gomorrah, the land was unfit to live
in, and Abraham moved outside the promised land into the land
of the Philistines. Satan acted to prevent Sarah from having
Abraham's child by causing the Philistine king, Abimelech, to
take her into his harem. We gather that Abimelech was seeking
children because his punishment was that all the wombs in his
household were closed (Gen. 20:18). Satan's hope was to get
Sarah pregnant by another man and thereby prevent the heir
from being born.

Abraham knew that there was no real fear of God in the land
of Philistia (Gen. 20:11), and Abimelech's action proved it. In
order to protect themselves when they went into a pagan land,
Abraham and Sarah would point to their brother-sister
relationship rather than their husband-wife relationship (Gen.
20:2, 12). This was because in the ancient cultures the brother
was the sister's especial protector, and no one would have laid
a hand on Sarah without seeking Abraham's permission.[5]
Abraham could protect her by refusing such permission. That

---

[5] On the brother's special position as protector of the sister, see Genesis 24:29–31, 50,
60; Genesis 34; 2 Samuel 13.

Abimelech seized Sarah showed that he did not respect either God or custom.

Abraham had only one recourse left: prayer. God was pleased to hear and answer him, for "the effective supplication of a righteous man can accomplish much" (Jas. 5:16). God appeared to Abimelech and threatened to kill him, and Abimelech returned Sarah. More than that, Abimelech was told that only Abraham's prayers would remove the plague from his household (Gen. 20:7, 17–18). We see from this that prevailing prayer is one of the marks of true, patient faith.

Another of the blessings of patient faith is seen here. In Genesis 12, when Pharaoh attacked Sarai and God plagued him, he did not repent but drove Abram out. This time the tyrant did repent. He turned to the true God and asked Abraham to pray for him. He invited Abraham to remain in the land, offering him the best part (Gen. 20:15). He made a covenant with Abraham and allowed Abraham to establish true worship in his land (Gen. 21:22–34, esp. 33). In this way God rewarded Abraham's patience by giving him a restful land to live in (though not the promised land) and a healthy spiritual environment in which to rear his coming son.

By taking Abraham through these trials God was training him to take a long view—an epic view. He would inherit the land, but only after four hundred years of sojourning outside it, beginning with his move out of Canaan into Philistine territory. He would not personally inherit it, so he would have to train his sons in such a way that they could train their sons for generations (Gen. 18:19). He would have to teach them the word of God. He would have to establish sound patterns, habits, and rituals for them. And he would have to be near to them, comforting them so that they might learn to comfort others. In short, he would have to be a pastor to his family and set up patterns of life that would carry down through the generations.

Such long-term, patient endurance in well-doing would, he knew, be rewarded.

Abraham learned to see the entire future of his "multitude of sons" through the lens of the one son, Isaac. When God called on him to offer Isaac as a sacrifice, Abraham went to do so, confident that God would have to keep His promise and thus would raise Isaac from the dead (Gen. 22:5 says "we will return to you"). He knew that he had a full quiver even with only one son (Ps. 127). Like the parents of Samson, he knew that it was the quality of his children, not the sheer number of them, that made for a full quiver.

Yet God had a surprise in store for Abraham. When Sarah died at the age of 127, Abraham was 137 years old (Gen. 17:17; 23:1). A few years later, Abraham married a second time, to Keturah, and then he lived another thirty-five or so years (Gen. 25:1–7). In his second marriage Abraham had six sons, each of whom became the father of an important nation of people (Gen. 25:2–4). Thus, after many years of patient faith, Abraham received a fulfillment of the promise in terms he had come not to expect.

Patience and Name

A person's name in the Bible has to do with his character and glory. The builders of the Tower of Babel had sought to make themselves a "name," and God thwarted them (Gen. 11:4). God told Abram that if he remained patient, He would bestow on him a "name."

The name was at first "Exalted Father," and then later "Father of a Multitude." While this name implies many heirs, it also implies glory and a position of preeminence and rule over other "sons," as we see when Joseph calls himself a father of Pharaoh (Gen. 45:8). It is a name that speaks of the kind of privilege Adam would have gained had he not sinned.

As we read the story we can see God magnifying Abraham's influence over the years. Abraham was already an important sheik when he moved into Canaan. Based on the number of fighting men in his personal army (Gen. 14:14), some scholars have estimated that his household would have contained at least 3,000 persons, and perhaps as many as 10,000. We should not be fooled by the fact that Abraham lived in tents, for such tents were not teepees or mere affairs of cloth and post. The Tabernacle of Yahweh was such a house-tent, and while it was portable, it had wooden walls with separate and very large rooms.

Abraham's influence came through his witness to the true God. He started by building altars and making converts. By the time we get to the story of the capture of Lot we see that several important sheiks have become converts and thus allies of Abram (Gen. 14:13). After Abram's victory over Chedorlaomer, even the king of Sodom treated him with respect and offered him all the spoils (Gen. 14:21).

Abraham's elevation continues in chapters 18 and 20. In Genesis 20:7, Abraham is called a "prophet." We are used to thinking of a prophet as someone who hears and then proclaims God's word, and this is true as far as it goes. The person who only sees and proclaims, however, is a "seer," not a full "prophet." A prophet is a member of God's council, and he is actually consulted during deliberations. The prophet is invited to speak, and God listens to his advice (Amos 3:7; 7:2–3, 5–6).

Adam was positioned originally as a seer, one who heard God's word and was to teach it to his wife. Had he been faithful, he would have become a prophet, someone taken into God's counsel. Abraham's privilege as a council member is seen in the familiar story in Genesis 18, when God asks his advice about the destruction of Sodom and Abraham persuades God not to destroy the city if there are ten righteous persons in it. In this story we see that, as a reward for his patient faith, Abraham received a great name with God.

In Genesis 23, we see the greatness of his name with men. Abraham needed a burial plot for Sarah, and the place he needed to bury her was in Hittite territory. The Hittites had been converted by Abraham and viewed him as a "Prince of God" (Gen. 23:6), that is, a leader in God's kingdom. They wanted to honor him by giving him the land he needed, but Abraham refused to receive even a small plot of the promised land as a gift from men. Instead, he insisted on using the money God had given him to purchase the land (Gen. 23:6–16). The story shows the high esteem in which the Hittites held Abraham and their desire to honor him in any way possible.

Conclusion

An abiding temptation before all men, ever since Adam, is to seize at privileges and prerogatives, rather than wait for them to be bestowed. Jesus warned about this in a parable, recorded in Luke 14:7–11.

> And He began speaking a parable to the invited guests when He noticed how they had been picking out the places of honor at the table, saying to them, 'When you are invited by someone to a wedding feast, do not take the place of honor, lest someone more distinguished than you may have been invited by him, and he who invited you both shall come and say to you, "Give place to this man," and then in disgrace you proceed to occupy the last place. But when you are invited, go and recline at the last place, so that when the one who has invited you comes, he may say to you, "Friend, move up higher"; then you will have honor in the sight of all who recline at table with you. *For everyone who exalts himself shall be humbled, and he who humbles himself shall be exalted.*'

The story of Abraham is God's great encouragement to us

along these lines. He was given great promises: heirs, inheritance, and heritage.[6] Yet, years went by and it seemed that those promises would never be fulfilled. All the same, despite many trials, God continued to take care of Abraham, and Abraham continued in humility and refused to try and seize the blessings. He waited on the Lord and only lapsed on one occasion. Even that lapse is an encouragement, for who among us has not failed at patience?

Whether in the church, in business, or in some other enterprise, the impatient man often seizes glory and leadership first. Such "driven men," however, burn out after a while and are forced to take a lower place. The faithful, patient man is encouraged by the story of Abraham. He is building for the future, and even if the blessing does not come in his lifetime, he has the joy of knowing that the reward of patient faith will be his.

[6] The heir is the seed, the inheritance is the land, and the heritage, Abraham's great name that would be a blessing to all peoples, is ultimately the Lord Himself.

6 FAITH AND COMMUNITY

The Story of Lot

If the story of Abraham encourages us to patience, the story of Lot shows us the consequences of impatience and also of forsaking the Christian community for the world. Though it is a depressing story, it does give us hope. For in spite of his mistakes, Lot was a righteous man, and his spirit was vexed by the evil in Sodom (2 Pet. 2:7). God did not abandon this man but delivered him and gave him new opportunities to live in community with the faithful. Sadly, Lot did not avail himself of these.

The story of Lot can be seen as four exoduses: an exodus from Ur and Haran, an exodus from Egypt, a deliverance from Chedorlaomer, and an exodus from Sodom. As we look at these, we find the clues to Lot's faith and to his compromises.

Lot's First and Second Deliverances

An exodus is a deliverance. There are many exoduses in Scripture, the most prominent being the exodus of the nation of Israel from Egypt. In the book of Genesis we read of several exoduses, each of which shows the people of God being delivered from bondage into the promised land. The first of these is recorded in Genesis 11:31–12:5. It records how God appeared to Abram and his family and told them to leave Ur of the Chaldeans. The family converted to Yahweh and departed this pagan city (Josh. 24:2), moving to Haran with their property. A few years later they moved on from Haran to Canaan, arriving with great possessions and a community of converts. Lot, Abram's nephew, came with the family.

They prospered in the land until God brought a famine. Just as a famine later drove Jacob into Egypt, so this famine drove

Abram and Lot into Egypt (Gen. 12:10–20). Pharaoh attacked God's people, God struck him with plagues, and God's people, in this case Abram and Lot, escaped with much spoil—the same as happened later on when the Israelites left Egypt.

Once they were back in the land, problems developed between Lot and Abram. We read in Genesis 13:5–7: "Now Lot, who went with Abram, also had flocks and herds and tents. And the land could not bear them to dwell together; for their possessions were so great that they were not able to remain together. And there was strife between the herdsmen of Abram's livestock and the herdsmen of Lot's livestock." At this point, the writer of Genesis inserts a comment: "Now the Canaanite and the Perizzite were dwelling then in the land."

To understand this passage, we have to keep in mind that the herdsmen would not have gotten into conflict unless their leaders were in conflict to some degree. Abram was in command of the sheikdom. He had no conflict with Lot. If there was a conflict, it was Lot who was largely to blame. The land God had given them was sufficient, and there was plenty for all, *unless some were overly ambitious.* James comments that "where jealousy and selfish ambition exist, there is disorder and every evil thing" (Jas. 3:16). It was Lot who chafed under Abram's leadership, but instead of seeking new lands for himself, he permitted conflict to erupt between his men and those of the sheik.

This is partly why the writer inserts the comment about the Canaanite living in the land. One aspect of his intention is to show that other people were crowding Abram and Lot for the available land. But we should also see that Lot and his people were living like Canaanites, those who had inherited the mentality of rebellious Ham. If Lot was not careful, he would wind up under the judgment of Canaan. Sadly, that is what happened.

Abram graciously sought peace. He possessed the "wisdom from above, which is first pure, then peaceable, gentle, reasonable" (Jas. 3:17). He pointed out to Lot that the land was plenty big enough for them both and invited Lot to take first choice. Abram would take what was left (Gen. 13:8–9). Lot chose an area that looked attractive, for it was like the Garden of Eden (Gen. 13:10). He overlooked the fact that the city of Sodom, like the forbidden tree, was erected in the middle of this garden, and he "moved his tents as far as Sodom" (Gen. 13:12).

Lot had made a grave mistake. It was not wrong to seek for a good land, but it was wrong to forsake the community of the faithful in order to do so. Abram had suggested Lot choose the right hand or the left, which is south or north (Gen. 13:9). Lot chose east, a direction not commended by Abram, and one that is sometimes both morally and symbolically suspect in the book of Genesis (Gen. 4:16; 11:2). Abram had invited Lot to "keep in touch." Instead, Lot moved far away. The writer of Genesis comments immediately: "Now the men of Sodom were wicked and sinners exceedingly against Yahweh" (Gen. 13:13). Lot had chafed under godly authority. He had been given a gracious offer, but he had made a foolish choice. Seeking prosperity, he had moved in with Canaanites, but he had not demonstrated sufficient wisdom to handle the situation.

Even so, God would prove gracious to him and not forget him.

Lot's Third Deliverance

When Sodom rebelled against Chedorlaomer, the latter invaded Canaan, conquered all the rebels, and captured much of the populace of Sodom. None of this particularly interested Abram until he heard that Lot had been captured along with the rest. Abram immediately gathered his troops and set out to rescue Lot (Gen. 14:11–16).

With a mighty hand Abram delivered Lot from bondage, punished the enemy, and returned with much spoil. He also brought out of bondage a "mixed multitude" of Canaanites. These he returned to Sodom, refusing any of the spoil.

Abram's refusal of the king of Sodom's offer stands in contrast to Lot's acceptance of that king's hospitality. While we read nothing else about Lot in this passage, we are to understand that he has been given an opportunity to rejoin the covenant community. Sodom had not been able to protect him from capture. Rather, it was God's man, Abram, who had shown himself to be Lot's protector. Would Lot follow Abram's lead and reject Sodom? Would Lot reaffiliate with Abram and come under his leadership?

Sadly, he chose Sodom, again!

Lot's Fourth Deliverance

There came a time when the iniquity of the Sodomites was so great that God determined to investigate them with a view to destroying them if they merited it. He sent two angelic witnesses to examine conditions and report back to Him. Meanwhile, God disclosed His plan to Abram and solicited his prophetic comments (Gen. 18:16–22). God did not have to include Abram in His deliberations, but He chose to do so in order to train Abram in righteousness.

Abram asked God, "Will You really sweep away the righteous with the wicked?" (Gen. 18:23). Suppose there are fifty righteous, Abram wanted to know. Would God destroy the city if there werre fifty righteous people in it? No, God would not.

Abram and God continued their conversation until God promised not to destroy the city even if there were ten righteous people in it (Gen. 18:32). Abram had been working to this point because he knew that Lot had at least two sons, two married daughters and two sons-in-law, two unmarried daughters, and a wife, for a total of ten (Gen. 18:12, 14, 15). Abram figured Lot would be safe.

This brings a question to our minds. Certainly many times the righteous suffer right along with the wicked. Why does God promise here that it shall not be so? What is unique about this situation? The answer is that the judgment of Sodom is an example of a final judgment. In terms of final judgment, God never destroys the righteous with the wicked. Abraham talked God down to ten, but then he realized the truth that God was trying to get through to him: Even if there is only one, God does not destroy the righteous with the wicked. God *removes* the righteous first. There must be an exodus before the final judgment falls.

The two angels arrived at Sodom. Their plan was to camp out in the city square and there evaluate the city, but Lot persuaded them that this would be dangerous and brought them to his house (Gen. 19:2–3). Lot himself was sitting in the gate of the city, which indicates that he was a man of prominence in Sodom, for that is where judges sat (Gen. 19:1, 9). There is a parallel here with Abraham. Abraham was growing greater and greater in God's eyes and getting a greater and greater name as a result of his patient faithfulness. Lot had also grown to importance, but in Sodom. His "name" would not endure. His magnitude was an illusion.

It happened that Lot served the angels unleavened bread (Gen. 19:3). Later, when Israel was delivered from Egypt, God commanded them to use unleavened bread. This was in part to remind them of Lot. They were being delivered from Egypt as Lot had been delivered from Sodom. They were to learn from the sad mistake Lot made after his exodus. Unfortunately, they chose to repeat his errors.

Later in the evening men from every quarter of the city, without exception, came and tried to attack the two angelic witnesses. Lot offered his daughters to them instead, but they refused them. Lot's family was delivered when the angels miraculously dazzled the eyes of the Sodomites and they were unable to find Lot's door. Lot's offering of his daughters is an example of the kind of predicament good people can get into if they foolishly choose to live in a wicked environment.

The angels realized that God would destroy Sodom in the morning. They encouraged Lot to gather his family and leave. Sadly, Lot's sons would not listen to him and neither would his married daughters and their husbands. All were lost. When morning came and the Day of the Lord arrived, the angels exhorted Lot to go, "but he hesitated" (Gen. 19:16). His discernment was greatly muddied after his years in Sodom. God showed him grace, however, and the angels "seized his hand" and led him out of the city.

It is important to notice that the angels told Lot to escape to "the mountain" (Gen. 19:17, 19). This command is pregnant with associations. The Garden of Eden was on a mountain. Later, when Israel was called from Egypt, they were taken straight to a Mountain of God. In context, moreover, the angels were telling Lot to return to Abraham. It was while living on a mountain that Lot and Abraham had separated (Gen. 12:8; 13:3), and at the time of Sodom's destruction, Abraham was living nearby at Hebron, on a mountain (Gen. 19:27–28).

Lot, however, did not trust the word of the Lord. He was convinced that he could not reach the mountain in time and asked to be permitted to go only to a small neighboring town, which he was allowed to do. By failing to rejoin Abraham, Lot lost his last opportunity for earthly grace (Gen. 19:19–22). This was Lot's last exodus. Because he failed to rejoin Abraham, he lived the rest of his life in the wilderness. The same sad story was played out again when God delivered Israel from Egypt under Moses.

Living in Death

After living in Zoar for a while, Lot moved to the mountain, but Abraham had already moved away and gone to Gerar (Philistia, Genesis 19:30; 20:1). The mountain had been abandoned and was no longer a place of grace or honor for Lot. Instead of following Abraham to Gerar, Lot chose to stay far from him. Instead of dwelling in tents, he lived in a cave.

In the Bible, hiding in a cave is a sign of being close to death. When the enemy is near, you take refuge in pits and caves. To live in a cave is to live in death. God had said, "you are dust, and to dust you shall return" (Gen. 3:19). Insertion into the dust of the earth—burial—is the sign of death. Abraham buried Sarah in a cave (Gen. 23:19). Jesus was also buried in a cave. Lot was returning to dust, living in death. His poor choices and his failure to live in community with God's people led him to this horrid plight.

When Adam named the animals he found no helper fit to be his companion. As we saw in chapter one, Eve was brought to Adam to establish the community of faith. It is fitting that one consequence of Lot's forsaking the covenant community was the loss of his wife. There can be no lasting community, even of marriage, outside the faith.

Lot's failure to live in community with the faithful had another grievous result: There were no young men for his daughters to marry. The daughters thus hit upon a plan to get their father drunk and then lie with him in order to produce offspring. Parent-child incest had been strictly forbidden from the beginning, as Adam had recognized when he said, "For this cause a man shall leave his father and mother and shall cleave to his wife" (Gen. 2:24). If marriage involves leaving parents, it cannot involve marrying them! The daughters either did not know this or did not care. Either way, Lot's training of them was clearly deficient.

There are deliberate parallels here to the story of Ham. Noah had drunk wine to celebrate his deliverance, but Lot drank in order to forget. Noah was not in a stupor, for he knew what Ham had done, but Lot drank himself into oblivion. In both cases a sinful child invaded the father's privacy, uncovered his nakedness (in different senses), and seized something forbidden. In both cases the judgment was that their children would live under a curse. Ham's son Canaan would be cursed because he would follow in his father's footsteps. Similarly, the grandchildren of Lot would become just like Canaanites, for Lot and his daughters had absorbed the culture and ways of Canaan.

The children born of this unnatural union became two of the greatest of Israel's enemies: the Moabites and the Ammonites. They were so wicked that the only nations they could be compared with were Sodom and Gomorrah, which was no surprise since from their beginnings they had been perpetuating that cursed culture (Zeph. 2:8–10).

Conclusion

Such was the sad legacy of Lot. Abraham lived as an alien in the land of promise, looking for a city whose architect and builder is God (Heb. 11:9–10). Lot looked to the nearby city of Sodom and lost sight of the city of God. For twenty years it appeared that Lot was prospering in the Cainite city, but the end was death. Lot moved himself into the tents of Canaan and received the judgment of Ham.

Abraham gradually became well known to the men of his day and ascended to greatness in their eyes because he put Yahweh and His ways first. Lot sought a shortcut and became a judge in Sodom, but it did not endure.

Abraham trained his children with a view to the conquest of Canaan four hundred years later, and in spite of their sins, they were a worthy company. Lot's descendants simply carried the culture of Ham-Canaan-Sodom into the future and eventually had to be destroyed.

The story of Lot is a forbidding one. It warns young men not to seize the prerogatives of older men. More importantly, it warns us not to forsake the Christian community in the interest of any other enterprise. As depressing as it is, however, the story of Lot is not just a negative warning. It is also filled with hope, for in spite of his sins, God repeatedly delivered Lot, giving him one opportunity after another. May God do the same for us!

7   FAITH AND TYRANNY
The Stories of Isaac and Rebekah

The man who seizes forbidden fruit seeks to make himself a god. Since the Fall, men have tended to become tyrants, seizing power and lording it over other people. In the nature of the case, such tyrants appear on the scene of human history first. Why? Because the saints are required to go through years of patient, wisdom-inducing difficulties before God gives them the privilege to rule. In the meantime the wicked, having seized power, dominate society.

Because of this, the Bible has a great deal to say about how faith operates in a context of tyranny. Speaking of tyrants, Jesus tells us that if we are forced to go one mile we should go another and thus win favor and a hearing for God's Word (Mt. 5:41). Paul tells us to render them taxes and honor so that they will leave us in peace while we undermine them with the gospel (Rom. 13:1–7). Paul also tells us to pray for them that they might be converted and rule charitably (1 Tim. 2:2).

Tyranny and how to avoid it are two of the major themes in Genesis. The basic world tyranny was set up at the Tower of Babel. God scattered the people and prevented the development of a one-world power state, but this did not stop the erection of many smaller tyrannies. Abraham had to contend with tyrants in Egypt and Philistia. Isaac had to contend with a Philistine tyrant and then became a tyrant himself. Jacob was tyrannized by his father Isaac, by his brother Esau, and by his uncle Laban. Finally, Joseph was used by God to convert the tyrant of Egypt into a true and godly ruler.

Deceiving Tyrants

The basic means for dealing with tyrants in Genesis, and in the rest of Scripture, is through deception. The reason for this goes back to the garden. The serpent tricked Eve through deception (Gen. 3:13; 2 Cor. 11:3; 1 Tim. 2:14) while Adam stood by and failed to protect her. Accordingly, a theme emerges later in Scripture wherein the serpent attacks the bride and the husband must attempt to protect her. In each case it is the intention of the serpent to use the bride to raise up his own seed.[1] In each case deception is used against the serpent as God acts to protect the bride.

The use of deception against the serpent is simply an application of the *lex talionis:* an eye for an eye, a tooth for a tooth, a deception for a deception. Jesus enjoins us to be "as wise as serpents, and as harmless as doves" because we have been sent out "as sheep among wolves" (Mt. 10:16). In other words, our practice of deception, where necessary, must be in order to further good and peace and never be a means of destroying our neighbor, for the ninth commandment forbids bearing false witness *against* our neighbor.

It is preeminently women or subordinates who practice deception in Scripture. Those in a vulnerable position who do not have power to engage in direct confrontation are advised to use deception and lies to evade the dragon. In addition to the examples we shall examine shortly in Genesis, we have the lies told by the Hebrew midwives in Exodus , and the deception practiced by Moses' mother in Exodus 2. We have the lie told

---

[1] That the serpent does have a seed is clear from Genesis 3:15, and this seed does come through the woman. Her hearkening to his voice was spiritually adulterous, and as a result both the satanic seed and the redeemed seed come through the woman. That which is essentially *hers,* however, is the community of the redeemed (Gen. 3:15). Thus the Pharisees were serpents, the offspring of the serpent (Mt. 23:33), for the serpent was their father (Jn. 8:44).

by Rahab in Joshua 2 and the deception by Jael in Judges 4 and 5.[2] Faced with the tyrant, the woman is not in a position to fight, but she can lie and deceive. It was the satanic tyrant in whose face these women told their brazen lies, and God blessed them each time for it (see the blessings in Gen. 12:16–17; 20:7, 14ff.; 26:12ff.; Exod. 1:20; Jas. 2:25; Mt. 1:5; Judg. 5:24).

Another instance of avoiding a tyrant by means of deception is provided by 1 Samuel 16:2, where we see that when Samuel feared the power of Saul, God Himself provided him with a deceptive strategy. Also note that David, when living among the Philistines, deceived them by feigning madness (1 Sam. 12:13–15; Ps. 34).

Because this biblical teaching will seem strange or even shocking to some readers, a few more words about it are in order before we look at examples in Genesis. I have found it helpful, building on Augustine and Luther, to distinguish five kinds of lies or deceptions. The first three are from Augustine (as recounted by Luther).[3]

First, *playful lies* are those told in jest or told by actors in the theater. Such lies do no harm and are even pleasing. Second, *obliging lies* are told to protect someone else. Augustine tells of a certain bishop who was unwilling to betray someone who had taken refuge with him. Dutch Christians lied to protect Jews and other oppressed minorities during the Nazi occupation of The Netherlands. Luther remarks that

> this lie is called 'obliging' because it not only serves the advantage of someone else, who would otherwise suffer harm or violence but also prevents a sin. Therefore it is not proper

---

[2] On Jael's lie and Deborah's praise for it see my book *Judges: A Practical and Theological Commentary* (Eugene: Wipf and Stock Publishers, [1985] 1999), pp. 84–90, 104.

[3] Martin Luther, *Lectures on Genesis,* in *Luther's Works* (St. Louis: Concordia), vol. 2 (1960), pp. 291f.; vol. 5 (1964), pp. 40f.

to call it a lie; for it is rather a virtue and outstanding pru-
dence, by which both the fury of Satan is hindered and the
honor, life, and advantages of others are served. For this
reason it can be called pious concern for the brethren, or, in
Paul's language, zeal for piety.[4]

The lies told by Abram and Isaac to protect their wives, and
by Rebekah to protect God's covenant with Jacob, were this sort
of "obliging" lie, and were entirely proper.[5]

The third kind of lie is the *destructive lie,* a violation of the
ninth commandment, designed to harm our neighbor. The
fourth kind of lie, which Luther does not mention, is *wartime
deception.* We could group this as a specimen of obliging lie,
but I have found it helpful to distinguish between deception as
a military tactic and the deception of a tyrant in the interest of
preserving life. The lie told by Jael at the battle of Megiddo is
an example of a praiseworthy military deception.

The fifth and last kind of lie or deception is that practiced
by a wise and godly person that leads up to a revelation and is
designed to shock a sinner into realizing his sin. This we may
call *evangelistic deception.* Jesus did this with the two people He
spoke with on the road to Emmaus (Lk. 24), because He allowed them to think He was just an ordinary man until just the
right moment. Joseph did the same thing with his brothers,
pretending to be an Egyptian tyrant until he had brought them
to repentance. The prophet Nathan told a lying story to David
in order to bring David to repentance (2 Sam. 12), as did the
wise woman of Tekoa (2 Sam. 14). As we shall see, this is the
kind of deception Rebekah and Jacob practiced on wicked Isaac,
and they were rewarded when that sinner repented.[6]

[4] *Ibid.,* p. 292.
[5] Luther exonerates Abram's and Isaac's deceptions as obliging lies. He finds Rebekah's
deception of Isaac more difficult but forcefully maintains that she was in the right all the
same. See his remarks on the relevant passages in *ibid.*
[6] I am indebted to the Rev. Eduardo Andrade of Good Shepherd Reformed Episcopal
Church, Brockton, Massachusetts, for the ideas and examples contained in this paragraph.

Let us now look briefly at Abraham's lies. In Genesis 12:10–20 we have the story of Abram and Sarai's deception of Pharaoh. As a result of a severe famine, Abram had moved to Egypt. He realized that Sarai's beauty would attract the unconverted Egyptians, and they might kill him and steal her. It is naive to discount Abram's fears. Homer's *Iliad* is all about such violent and adolescent cultures. The virtual "gang war" between the Aegeans and the Trojans came about when the Trojan prince Paris seized Helen, the beautiful wife of the Aegean Menelaos. Homer skillfully shows that the Aegeans were just as bad, for the *Iliad* begins by showing that the Aegeans had gone around grabbing all the pretty girls they could find and were refusing to give them up even when the gods themselves demanded that they do so. This is what pre-Christian, adolescent cultures are like, and Abram was absolutely right to take this fact into account and act upon it.

Abram knew that if he were killed Sarai's protection would be gone. Abram deceived Pharaoh by telling the Egyptians nothing more than that Sarai was his sister and not that she also was his wife. Abram counted on the common law of the ancient near east to protect Sarai, because any man desiring her would have to negotiate with her brother, and thus Abram would be able to forestall any marriage. The draconic Pharaoh, however, thinking himself a god, took Sarai without permission. As a result, God sent plagues against him. When Pharaoh found out what had happened, he assumed the role of satanic accuser and tried to pin the blame on Abram (as far too many people still do). Meanwhile, Abram had been prospered by God in his deception and emerged from Egypt with much spoil.

As we saw in chapter five, the same thing happened later on in Genesis 20. Again deception was Abraham's way of trying to avoid the tyrant. Abraham was not condemned by God for this; rather, it was Abimelech whose house was plagued. True, in neither of these stories was Abraham successful in avoiding the

tyrant, but that was because God had other purposes in mind.
God wanted Abram to come in contact with Pharaoh in order
to strike fear into Pharaoh and gain Abram much spoil. He
wanted Abraham to come in contact with Abimelech in order
to convert him to the faith. All the same, the strategy of avoiding tyrants and deceiving them where necessary is not condemned, and Abraham's use of this strategy is an example for
us.

Isaac and the Tyrant

Isaac's interaction with a new Abimelech, a new Philistine
tyrant, is found in Genesis 26. Once again a famine drove the
patriarch into the land of a pagan lord. Isaac told the Philistines that Rebekah was his sister and concealed the fact that she
was his wife. This was not actually a lie, but it was not the whole
truth either.

For us to understand this we have to grasp the biblical perspective. While Sarah physically was Abraham's sister, since both
had the same father (Gen. 20:12), Rebekah was Isaac's sister
by adoption. The brother-sister relationship is more fundamental than the husband-wife relationship, since it comes first. Eve
was Adam's sister before she became his wife. In the Song of
Solomon the woman is addressed as "my sister, my bride," never
the other way around (Song 4:9, 10, 12; 5:1, 2). Jesus tells us
that human marriage is only for time, not for eternity (Mt.
22:30). What endures forever is the brother-sister relationship.

Because of this, it was customary for a man to adopt a woman
as his sister at the same time he married her as a wife. For this
reason, negotiations for marriage were not conducted primarily with the girl's parents, but with her brother (Song 8:8). This
is seen in the story of Isaac and Rebekah: Abraham's servant ne-
gotiated with Rebekah's brother Laban, not with her father
Lemuel (Gen. 24:29–33, 50, 53, 55). Notice the wording of

Genesis 24:59–60, "Thus *they* sent away their *sister* Rebekah
. . . and they blessed Rebekah and said to her, 'May you, *our
sister.* . . .'"The most important aspect of the leaving and cleav-
ing was not that Rebekah was getting a husband but that she
was getting a new brother.

This passage clarifies the point made earlier respecting
Abraham's attempts to protect Sarah: In order to marry a
woman, you had to negotiate with her brother. By saying that
Rebekah was his sister, Isaac put himself in the best possible
position to protect them both. On the one hand, Isaac would
be safe. There would be no reason for anyone to kill him in order
to get Rebekah, because no one would know they were married. On the other hand, Rebekah would also be safe. Suitors
wishing to win her hand would have to negotiate with her
brother, and he could put them off indefinitely. God's covenant
would be safe, for Isaac would live to preach and perpetuate it.

God wanted Isaac to get close to Abimelech, however, and
so it came to pass that the king noticed that the relationship
between Isaac and Rebekah was clearly more than merely fra-
ternal and called Isaac to account for it. As in the stories about
Abraham, the king satanically tried to blame the righteous man,
but the accusation was rather ridiculous: "If one of the people
had raped her it would have been *your* fault for not telling us
she was your wife!" Abimelech had enough sense not to press
the matter and ordered that Isaac be protected (Gen. 26:8–11).

Isaac's troubles with the Philistine tyrants were not over, however. He was faced with their envy and their ability to shut him
down and drive him away. God was pleased with Isaac, and we
read that "Isaac sowed in that land and reaped in the same year
a hundredfold. And Yahweh blessed him, and the man became
rich and continued to grow richer until he became very wealthy;
for he had possessions of flocks and possessions of herds and a
great household, so that the Philistines envied him" (Gen.
26:12–14). The result was that the Philistines decided to drive

him out. They filled up his wells with dirt, and finally they asked him to leave (Gen. 26:15–16).

Isaac's wells were symbols of his ministry, just as Abraham's altars were symbols of his. Wells of water are reminders of the Garden of Eden, and throughout the Bible, they are signs of God's grace and blessing. By stopping up his wells the Philistines were trying to kill Isaac's ministry. So Isaac moved on and dug new wells (Gen. 26:18–20), but the Philistines stole these. Isaac moved on and set up his ministry yet again, at Sitnah, and dug a new well—and the Philistines stole it, too (Gen. 26:21). Finally God gave Isaac rest, and the new well at Rehoboth remained in his possession (Gen. 26:22).

In all this we see Isaac avoiding suicidal and revolutionary action. Had Isaac defied the powers, he would have lost everything. Through humility, deference, and a foregoing of his "rights," Isaac came to be a power in the community, and eventually the Philistines converted and allied with him (Gen. 26:23–33).

Isaac as the Tyrant

The story of Isaac takes an unexpected, all-too-common twist. Having survived the tyranny of others, Isaac himself becomes a tyrant, and the righteous are forced to deceive him in order to obey God.

Isaac had two sons. They were twins and struggled in the womb: the righteous Jacob against the wicked Esau. When Esau was born he was covered with hair, and he remained a hairy man all his life (Gen. 25:25; 27:11). There is nothing naturally bad about being a hairy man, but in the symbolism of the book of Genesis, Esau's hairiness pointed to his bestial nature—remember the meaning of God's clothing Adam with animal skins. When the two boys were grown, Esau became a skillful hunter, and in the context of Genesis this points back to Nimrod.

Jacob, by way of contrast, was a "perfect" man (Gen. 25:27). This word "perfect" is translated as "complete" or "peaceful" in some versions, but it means "righteously mature" and is the same word used for Noah in Genesis 6:9, for Abram in Genesis 17:1, and for Job in Job 1:1.

Jacob is one of the most commonly misunderstood and misinterpreted characters in the Bible, and we shall have to clear up his reputation as we go. At the outset we have to take seriously the fact that the Bible says he was righteously mature, and also the fact that had Jacob not been regenerate in the womb, he would not have fought with Esau.

From the beginning Jacob knew that he was appointed to inherit the covenant of God, because God had said so (Gen. 25:23). Esau was the first born of the twins, however, and so he stood to inherit the spiritual responsibilities of the family—the covenant—as a result. But Esau had no interest in the covenant, while Jacob desired it earnestly. There came a day when Jacob was able to test and prove Esau's carnality. Jacob knew that God had tested Adam with food and had told him to wait for a while before he would be allowed to eat of the Tree of Judicial Knowledge. Jacob, the wiser and more mature brother, determined to put the same test before Esau.

One day Esau came in from hunting. He was weary and hungry. Any one of the many servants in Isaac's household could have provided him a meal, but he was a man of no patience and was unwilling to wait the half hour it might have taken to prepare a meal. Jacob had cooked a stew, and Esau asked for some. Jacob said, "Today sell me your birthright." On the face of it, this was a ridiculous demand. Esau should have said, "Forget it. I'll get food somewhere else." After all, Esau had come into the camp, and there were plenty of servants cooking pots of broth that he might have eaten. Instead the present-oriented

Esau said, "Behold, I am about to die; so of what use then is the
birthright to me?" The result was that Esau legally transferred
his birthright to Jacob by an oath (Gen. 25:29–34).

It seems incredible that Esau would accede to Jacob's bar-
gain. After all, he was not starving: Immediately after eating,
he hopped up and went his way—hardly the way a starving man
responds to his first meal in days. What the story shows is the
amazingly low esteem in which Esau held God's covenant and
blessings. To him they were nothing. The Bible's comment is
not "Thus Jacob stole Esau's birthright," but rather "Thus Esau
despised his birthright" (Gen. 25:34).[7]

Now Isaac knew about all this. He knew that God had said
Jacob was to inherit the covenant. He also knew that Esau had
legally signed it over to Jacob. Isaac, however, chose to turn a
blind eye to Jacob's and Esau's legal contract and to God's command.

The nature of Isaac's sin carries us back once again to the
garden, where Adam had been confronted with two trees, the
Tree of Life and the Tree of Judicial Knowledge. Both trees had
food, but one was forbidden. Isaac was confronted with two
sons, and these two sons also had food. It is helpful to remember, as we saw in chapter three, that the Bible often uses trees
and thorns as symbols of righteous and unrighteous men (Ps.
1; Judg. 9; Gen. 3:18; 4:1–2). Isaac had a choice between the
food that Jacob was providing by managing the household es-
tate (Gen. 25:27) and the food Esau was bringing in by drift-
ing around hunting all day. Like Adam, Isaac rejected God's
word and grew to prefer the forbidden son and his food (Gen.
25:28).

---

[7] It seems that Esau was particularly interested in what Jacob was cooking. Though it
was only lentil stew, Esau says, "Let me eat some of the red stuff, that red stuff" (25:30).
Some commentators note that God had forbidden men to drink blood after the flood; and
they suggest that blood was what Esau thought was in the pot.

As a result, Isaac became a tyrant. He determined to thwart God's statement regarding who was to inherit. He determined to break the legal transaction between Jacob and Esau. He determined to ignore the character and abilities of Jacob, the household manager, and chose instead to honor the shiftless Esau. By this time Esau had shown his contempt for God by taking two wives, neither of whom was in the covenant, and both of whom made life miserable for Isaac and Rebekah (Gen. 26:34–35). Esau had been married for years, and his sons were doubtless hellions like himself. This also Isaac determined to overlook. He intended to elevate the wicked and persecute the righteous.

Righteous Rebekah

Rebekah is the great heroine in the book of Genesis. Her very name is a play on the word "blessed," for in Hebrew the word for bless is written BRK, while Rebekah's name is written RBK. When we meet Rebekah in Genesis 24 she is like a new female Abram. As soon as she is given the opportunity to move to the promised land and join God's special people she cannot wait to do so. She refuses to stay with her old family a minute more than is necessary (Gen. 24:55–58).

The disdain with which Rebekah is treated by most Bible commentators and preachers is appalling. This is a woman who loved God, loved the covenant, and rightly loved the son who loved God and His covenant. She did not prefer Jacob for his food, but for himself (Gen. 25:28). For seventy-seven years (Gen. 8) she had observed Esau's sins and Jacob's faithfulness. And she also recognized what her sinning husband intended to do, for Isaac intended nothing less than the total destruction of God's covenant. Giving the covenant to Esau would eradicate everything that God had been doing. In God's wonderful providence, Rebekah just happened to be nearby when

Isaac announced his wicked plan to Esau. She determined to do something about it (Gen. 27:1–5).

Isaac called Esau and informed him that he was going to bestow the covenant and its blessings upon him. He asked Esau to go hunting and bring back some game to celebrate the event. (Notice the association with "forbidden" food again.) When Esau was gone, Rebekah told Jacob to deceive his father. Jacob was reluctant to do so, but Rebekah took all the consequences upon herself (Gen. 27:12–13). We see again that it is the woman who tricks the serpent, eye for eye and tooth for tooth. Even more importantly, we see that Rebekah was willing to die for the covenant. She offers her life and all her happiness to secure God's will. In her willingness to die Rebekah is nothing less than a picture of Jesus Himself.

The details are important. Isaac was, by this time, blind (Gen. 27:1). His physical blindness was a sign of his moral blindness. It is because tyrants are morally blind that they can be deceived.

Rebekah prepared a meal of clean, domestic food. This was the food associated with Jacob, and it was provided by Jacob (Gen. 27:9). Rebekah spiced the food to taste like one of Esau's dishes (Gen. 27:14). She then dressed Jacob in Esau's clothes, so that he would smell like Esau, placing animal skins on his arms and neck. Dressed in the skins of beasts, he resembled the hairy Esau (Gen. 27:15–16).

Jacob was able to allay Isaac's suspicions, and Isaac gave him the blessing. And what a blessing! The lawful procedure was for the firstborn to be given a double portion, with a single portion for the other son(s) (Deut. 21:17). Isaac, however, gave *everything* to the one he thought was Esau. We know this because when Esau returned and asked Isaac if he had reserved any blessing for the other son, Isaac replied, "Behold, I have made him your master, and all his brothers I have given to him for servants; and with grain and new wine I have sustained him. Now as for you, then, what can I do, my son?" (Gen. 27:37). Isaac had thought to deprive the godly Jacob of everything and reduce him to slavery under Esau. Instead, he did just the reverse. All he had left for Esau was a "blessing" that just might turn into a curse. He told Esau that one day he would break off his brother's yoke and be free of him; but like Lot when he departed from Abraham, Esau would find only death when he separated himself from Jacob and the covenant community.

In this way the tyranny of Isaac was evaded and the blessing came to God's people. And in this way, God showed grace to Isaac also, for when caught, Isaac repented and bowed before God's will, as we see from his renewed blessing of Jacob in Genesis 28:1.

Rebekah's plan worked. But what was her plan? Was Rebekah so ignorant as to think that unless Isaac gave the blessing, Jacob would not receive it? Did Rebekah think that Isaac could really thwart God's plan? No, not at all. If all Rebekah wanted to do was make sure that Jacob received the blessing, she did not have to do anything. She knew that God would take care of that. If Isaac destroyed the covenant, Rebekah knew that God could raise up Jacob as a new Abraham and start over. She was a woman of faith, not of superstition.

What Rebekah wanted was to shock and restore Isaac. That was her purpose, and God blessed it. After all, Isaac could have taken the blessing away from Jacob and given it to Esau. That would have been perfectly legitimate, since Jacob had received the blessing through deception. Surely if some stranger had disguised himself as Esau, Isaac could have cancelled his action. But Isaac had suspected that this "Esau" was really Jacob, and when he realized it, he bowed before God's mighty plan and repeated the blessing again in Genesis 28. (See Heb. 11:20, which says that Isaac's faith was restored and which refers to this second blessing.)

Conclusion

Throughout history God's people have lived under tyrannies. Since we are forbidden to seize the robe of authority and must wait for it to be bestowed, we are not permitted to engage in violent revolutionary action. Rather, we are enjoined to be patient and work to change society by the preaching of the gospel.

A strategy of avoiding conflict and confrontation with the "powers that be" is what the Bible always requires, except where the heart of the gospel is involved. The unconverted man, the tyrant, is primarily interested, after all, in power—that means the maintenance of force (through a drafted army) and the seizure of money (through taxation). If we think these are the most important things, then we will make them the point of resistance, becoming "tax patriots" or some such thing. To think this way is to think like pagans. For the Christian, the primary things are righteousness and diligent work. As often as not, the unconverted do not care how righteous we are or how hard we work, provided they get their tax money. This is why the Bible everywhere teaches us to go along with taxation, even when it is oppressive, and nowhere does it hint at the propriety of open tax resistance. The Christian has better things to spend time on, such as erecting altars and digging wells. Sometimes, of course, confrontation with the state cannot be avoided, such as when the civil authorities attack the church.

There are, of course, limits to the practice of deception. A case in point is found in the book of Esther. Mordecai, Esther's cousin, sought power with the king by telling Esther to conceal her faith (Est. 2:10, 20). This was a great evil, and God later forced Mordecai's hand over it, so that Esther was compelled to reveal her commitments. We note that Mordecai was a proud and vain man who refused to show deference to proper authorities (Est. 3:2; contrast Gen. 23:12; 33:3; 37:9–10). In this case

God protected the bride by converting (in some sense) her royal husband.[8] That God worked good out of Mordecai's pharisaical schemes in no way exonerates him, however, and this is clear in that he was forced to reverse his course. We see from this that deception of the tyrant must never involve denying the faith.

[8] Ahasuerus changes from being neutral toward the Jews to favoring them, conforming to the terms of the Abrahamic covenant. Whether this entailed personal salvation or not, we do not know. Unlike the case of Nebuchadnezzar (Dan. 4), we have no recorded prayer of confession from the lips of Ahasuerus.

8 FAITH AND ACCEPTANCE

The Story of Esau

We are so accustomed to what the New Testament says about Esau that we naturally think that he never came to faith. But what a couple of New Testament passages say is not the full story. Yes, Esau was a profane and godless man when he sold his birthright (Heb. 12:16–17), but did he never change?

God says, "Jacob I loved, but Esau I hated" (Mal. 1:26; Rom. 9:13), but hate does not have to mean pure hatred, undying hatred. In some passages "hate" means "to view as an enemy," as in Psalm 139:22. Jacob loved Rachel and hated Leah, but this only means he treated her as second-wife instead of as first-wife (Gen. 29:30–31). Jacob's "hatred" of Leah did not mean he divorced her and cast her out. Quite the contrary: He had many children by her, and Jacob honored her by burying her in the patriarchal tomb (Gen. 49:29–32). "Hate" in this case does not mean pure abiding hatred; it means to count as second, to prefer someone else as first. The same thing is meant when Jesus says we must hate our parents in order to love Him (Lk. 14:26). It means we place them second.

Certainly some passages of the Bible speak of hatred as an emotion of violent and total rejection. Paul's statement in Romans 9:13, however, is explained by the preceding verse: "'The elder shall serve the younger,' just as it is written, 'Jacob I loved and Esau I hated.'" It seems that God's hating Esau means no more than that He put Esau in second place. Paul goes on to use the Pharaoh of the exodus, not Esau, as the premier example of someone whose heart God chose in His sovereign plan to harden (Rom. 9:14ff).[1]

---

[1] Similarly, if all we read is Galatians 4:21–31, we might conclude that Ishmael was rejected by God. Yet Genesis says God made Ishmael His own child later on (Gen. 21:20, "God was with the lad"); and this was in answer to his parents' prayers (Gen. 16:11; 17:18–21; 21:12–13).

Many Bible readers do not realize that Job and at least some of his friends were descendants of Esau. Job lived in Uz, which was part of Edom, Esau's land (Job 1:1; Lam. 4:21). Teman, from which Eliphaz came, was also part of Edom (Job 2:11; Gen. 36:11). Though Eliphaz's faith was weak, he was saved in the end as Job prayed for him. We see from this that true faith was not absent from Esau's descendants later on.

Moreover, Caleb the Kenizzite was an Edomite, a descendant of Esau's grandson Kenaz (Gen. 36:11, 15; Num. 32:12; Joshua 14:6, 14). Caleb's younger brother was named Kenaz, and his son Othniel was the first of the judges of Israel (Josh. 15:17; Judg. 1:13; 3:9, 11). Caleb's grandson was also named Kenaz (1 Chr. 4:15). From all this we see that godly Edomites could rise to prominence in Israel. When Joshua and Caleb stand together as faithful spies and work together to conquer the land, we can see Jacob and Esau standing as brothers side by side.

Additionally, when Jacob returns to the land, Esau is already living in Mount Seir. According to Deuteronomy 2:22 and Joshua 24:4, Yahweh gave this land to Esau and drove out the Horites who lived there formerly. While this language might speak only of God's overall providence, it implies something more: that Esau had come to trust in Yahweh and that Yahweh acted on his behalf because of it.

But the most important evidence comes from Genesis 33. Esau had come out to meet Jacob with 400 men, and Jacob could only assume Esau was coming to kill him (Gen. 32:6). As it turns out, however, all Esau seems to have intended was to welcome Jacob and provide him an escort (Gen. 33:12–15). Possibly Esau originally did have bad intentions and then had a change of heart when he received all of Jacob's gifts (Gen. 32:13–21), but in fact the gifts don't seem to have been important to Esau. He was ready to give them back (Gen. 33:9–11).

We notice that "Esau ran to meet [Jacob] and embraced him, and fell on his neck and kissed him, and they wept" (Gen. 33:4). Clearly, not only was Esau no longer angry, but he was full of love for Jacob. Compare this with Luke 15:20, where the father runs to the prodigal son and embraces him in the same way.

When Esau initially rejected Jacob's gift, Jacob pressed him to take it. Jacob said that God had blessed him, and now he wanted to bless Esau. Esau was willing to receive this blessing from God through Jacob (Gen. 33:11).

Esau wanted Jacob to move to Seir and live with him. Far from shaking off a yoke with Jacob (Gen.27:40), Esau now desires it. Jacob refused Esau's offer, though he promised to visit him in his land of Seir later on (Gen. 33:14). Why? Is it because Esau was like Laban and wanted Jacob to serve him so that he would get more goodies from Jacob? It would not seem so, since Esau said, "I have plenty, my brother; let what you have be your own" (Gen. 33:9). Clearly Esau was not like Laban, and exploitation by Esau was not something Jacob needed to fear. Rather, Jacob knew that God's plan for him was to have his own place, so he could not join up with Esau and become part of Esau's kingdom.

It certainly looks as if Esau had become a changed man. We might see this as merely a psychological change, but given all that had gone before, I don't think we can limit it to that. Esau now recognizes that God is working through Jacob, and Esau is willing to receive God's blessings through Jacob.

Esau's faith is seen in his submission to the plan of God. He has come to accept the fact that though God may decide to elevate Jacob above him, yet God has blessings for him also. Esau no longer grasps for forbidden fruit.

Rebekah's Prayers

When Rebekah deceived Isaac she was not only trying to get him to do what was right, but she was also offering a prayer. She was praying that God would restore her husband to His grace. And God answered her prayer.

Her actions were also a prayer that both of her sons would be blessed. We can see this in the way she ritually combined both her sons together when she sent Jacob in to deceive Isaac. First, she took two kids of the goats, not one, and combined them into one meal.[2] Second, while the essence of the meal was the two kids—Jacob's domestic food, not Esau's game, but the spices added were Esau's spices. Third, she put Esau's clothes on Jacob, so that Jacob carried Esau with him into Isaac's presence, just as Jacob's food carried Esau's spices. Rebekah's prayer was that Esau would be carried by Jacob's faithfulness throughout his life, that the blessing that came upon Jacob would also come upon Esau.

It is clear that God answered her prayer. The future that God had planned for Jacob also became Esau's future. As God would eventually drive out the Canaanites for Jacob, so God drove out the Horites from Seir for Esau. Just as Jacob would receive a good inheritance, so also did Esau. And all the evidence suggests that just as Jacob learned to trust God more and more, so Esau came to trust Him as well.

All because of a mother's prayer.

---

[2] Joseph's supposed death is signified by the blood of a goat, a kid (37:31). Judah sent a kid of the goats to Tamar, which unbeknownst to him, signified the child(ren) he also "sent" to her (38:17–20). On goat-kids as human kids, see also Exodus 23:19; 34:26; Deuteronomy 14:21; Lamentations 4:10; 2 Kings 6:28f.; Judges 15:1.

Conclusion

Is Esau in heaven? I'm not sure we have quite enough to go on to be certain. But it does appear likely, and given the prayers of righteous Rebekah, who loved both her sons and prayed for them for years, I believe he is. We should take heart from this fact and believe that however many years it may take, God will answer the prayers of parents and the prodigal son will return.

9   FAITH AND WRESTLING

The Story of Jacob

After Isaac blessed Jacob, he sent him to his relative Laban in Padan Aram to get a wife. Jacob lived with Laban for twenty difficult years before finally escaping from his control. As he approached the promised land, he heard that Esau was coming out to meet him. Fearing the worst, he took steps to protect his family and sent them across the river. He himself remained alone on the other side of the Jabbok river, just outside the promised land (Gen. 32:22–24; Deut. 3:16; Josh. 12:2).

During the night, when it was dark and Jacob could not see, he was attacked by someone who wrestled with him until daybreak. Jacob was unable to identify this man. He only knew that he was being assaulted and had to defend himself. It was not an easy task for a man of ninety-seven years![1]

Who could it be? It is not too hard for us to imagine what went through Jacob's mind during the night. Perhaps his first thought was that it was his father Isaac. Isaac was a spry 157 years old, and he still had another twenty-three years to go (Gen. 25:26; 35:28). "My father is blind," Jacob thought, "and he has come to fight me on equal terms. I have less advantage over him in this darkness."

Jacob cast his mind back over the years. "It started when Esau and I were about twenty years old. Father turned away from

---

[1] "Joseph was 30 years of age when he stood before Pharaoh (Gen. 41:46). Hence at the end of the seven years of plenty he was 37, and after two years of famine, when Jacob himself was 130 (Gen. 47:9), he (Joseph) was 39 years of age. Therefore, since Joseph was 39 when his father Jacob was 130, the latter was 91 at the birth of Joseph. Now Jacob had served Laban 14 years when Joseph was born (Gen. 30:25). Therefore, Jacob was 77 when he came to Padan Aram and entered the service of Laban." Philip Mauro, *The Wonders of Bible Chronology* (Swengel, PA: Reiner Pub., 1970), p. 29. Jacob served Laban for six more years (Gen. 31:41), reaching the age of 97 when he returned to Canaan.

me and preferred him. There were fifty-seven years of being treated as second rate, until I finally left home twenty years ago. Fifty-seven years of being despised, in spite of all my careful work and management of the household. Fifty-seven years of having to wrestle with father for every crumb of attention and praise, while he lavished his affection on worthless Esau. Fifty-seven long, bitter years of patient struggle."

"He never wanted to give me any inheritance at all. I've been gone for twenty years, and now he's come to prevent my return. He still wants Esau to have it, and so he's stopped me at the border. Will he never leave me alone? Will I always have to wrestle with my own father?"

Such were Jacob's thoughts. Yet, as the minutes wore on, Jacob began to realize that this could not be Isaac. Isaac simply would not be able to sustain energy for so long a time, not at 157 years of age. It had to be someone else.

"Esau! Of course! Esau said he would kill me. That's why I had to leave home so hurriedly. I'd hoped he'd forgotten by now; after all, he doesn't think much beyond the present moment. But here he's come out with four hundred men, and you don't bring along an army of four hundred men just to say hello" (Gen. 27:41–43; 32:6).

"Wrestling with Esau! I've been doing that for longer than I can remember. We started fighting while we were still in the womb. He never cared for God, and I did, so we were enemies from the start. Our struggle lasted seventy-eight years, and now it's starting again."

Jacob had tried to buy Esau off. He had selected a huge gift for him and sent it to him in nine separate packages. He had spaced the gifts out so that Esau would receive them one at a time and be amazed and delighted with each new peace offering (Gen. 32:13–20). He remembered Esau as a carnal man and had hoped that the bribes would work.

Yet, as the minutes went by, Jacob began to wonder. "Esau really should have been bought off by my gifts. And I don't hear any sound of war from across the river. My camp is not being attacked. Maybe this is not Esau after all. And if it's not, there is only one other possibility.

"Laban!"

Laban

When Jacob arrived in Padan Aram, Laban welcomed him as a brother, saying "Surely you are my bone and my flesh" (Gen. 29:14). After a month, however, Laban decided to take advantage of this poor relation. "Are you my brother?" he asked, thus repudiating any claim Jacob might have. "You don't want to serve me for nothing, so tell me what your wages should be."[2]

Harold Stiger's remarks on Laban the tyrant are to the point: "One must not think that it was out of any largess that Laban made his offer. His constant change of Jacob's wages (Gen. 31:41) and his selling of his daughters and using up what was theirs (Gen. 31:15) work against this view. He was out to obtain every advantage in using Jacob for his own purposes. But in this instance Jacob was 'trapped' by his own love for Rachel. His love and his poverty made him vulnerable. On the other hand, if he had hired out to another in Haran, would Rachel have been available at the end of his time when he had acquired enough to pay the dowry? Thus Jacob finds himself in the grip of circumstances he cannot avoid."[3]

Laban is revealed to us as a shrewd and vicious man who had Jacob in a vise and intended to make use of him in every way possible. He deceived Jacob with regard to Rachel, giving him

[2] This is a preferable translation of Genesis 29:15, according to the research of David Daube and Reuven Yaron, "Jacob's Reception by Laban," *Journal of Semitic Studies* I (1956):60–62. The authors point out that a family member would not have worked for wages and so Laban here excluded Jacob from the family.

[3] Harold G. Stigers, *A Commentary on Genesis* (Grand Rapids: Zondervan, 1976), p. 229f.

Leah instead, and forced Jacob to work another seven years (Gen. 29:21–30). During these fourteen years, Jacob had nothing. He was paid no wages. He lived as a slave. His only benefits were his wives and whatever gifts Laban deigned to give him.

Laban's deception of Jacob is the opposite of what we saw in chapter seven. Jacob was no tyrant, and Laban had no reason to deceive him, except out of cruelty and oppression. Laban's lies were like those of Satan, the father of lies.

After fourteen years of bondage Jacob was ready to leave Laban. Laban realized that God had prospered him because of Jacob, and so Laban cut another deal with him. "Why go home empty-handed? Stay on with me and work. Name your wages." So a deal was cut. Laban, however, refused to honor it. Repeatedly during the next six years he changed Jacob's wages. He also held back all the inheritance his daughters were to receive and used it up (Gen. 31:7, 15). Jacob decided to leave.

He knew, however, that Laban would not permit it. Jacob was a goose who laid golden eggs, and Laban intended to keep him. So Jacob waited until Laban left on a three-day journey to visit his own flock, and then he fled as fast as he could (Gen. 30:36; 31:17–22).

Jacob's worries were well founded, for Laban did indeed pursue him. It took him seven days to catch up with Jacob, and doubtless he would have done him harm if God had not intervened. In a dream God told Laban, "Take heed to yourself that you do not speak to Jacob either good or evil" (Gen. 31:24). As we have seen, knowing good and evil refers to judicial knowledge, and in this case, "speaking good and evil" refers to passing and enforcing judgment. God told Laban that Jacob was not under his authority; Laban had better not try to rule him or judge him (Gen. 31:29).

Thus cowed, Laban could do nothing but accuse and complain. He accused Jacob of deceiving him (Gen. 31:26). He accused Jacob of stealing his daughters and his property, though Jacob had earned all of it (Gen. 31:43). Then Laban assumed a proud posture and magnanimously forgave Jacob for robbing him, saying that after all he did not want to bring harm to his daughters and grandchildren (Gen. 31:43). He suggested that they make a covenant and establish peace between themselves, which they did (Gen. 31:44–55).

But how trustworthy was Laban? Had he ever kept his word? No. So it was entirely likely that Laban had returned in the dead of night to settle his affairs with Jacob by killing him. After all, no one would know.

Jacob had wrestled with Esau all his life. He had wrestled with his father all his adult life. He had wrestled with Laban for twenty years. It could have been any of these three who attacked him that night, but it wasn't.

It was God with whom Jacob had to do.

Wrestling with God

As the dawn began to break, the person with whom Jacob wrestled "touched the socket of his thigh; so the socket of Jacob's thigh was dislocated while he wrestled with him" (Gen. 32:25). Jacob then realized that he had been wrestling with God. God— the Angel of Yahweh—said "Let Me go, for the dawn is breaking," but Jacob refused to let go until he had been blessed. So God said, "Your name shall no longer be Jacob [One Who Supplants Another (by wrestling)], but Israel [One Who Strives With God (by wrestling)]; for you have striven [as Israel] with God and [as Jacob] with men, and you have prevailed" (Gen. 33:28).

Why was God wrestling with Jacob? Was it because Jacob was a wicked man, so that God was seeking to overpower him, to bring him to his knees? If such were the meaning of the story, then why does God say that Jacob has prevailed? We should expect then, in this interpretation, to see God prevail by defeating Jacob and then bringing him to repentance. Such an interpretation does not fit the story.

As we have seen, the Bible presents Jacob as a righteous man even in the womb and as a mature believer for his entire life: a "perfect" man. God had spoken to him and made promises to him twenty years earlier at Bethel (Gen. 28:10–22), showing again that he was already accounted righteous. The very day before this night of wrestling, Jacob had labored—wrestled—in prayer to his God (Gen. 32:9–12). Thus, Jacob was no carnal, unconverted man whom God had to beat into shape; nor was his experience at Peniel his conversion. Something else entirely is in view.

The message of Peniel is this: It was God who raised up Esau, Isaac, and Laban to wrestle with Jacob. All those years when Jacob wrestled with these three enemies, it was really God with whom he had to do. And why? Not to punish Jacob, but to train him, to make him strong.

Just as a father gets down on the floor and wrestles with his children, so God had wrestled with Jacob. Just as a father sets hard tasks before his children to train them for adult responsibilities, so God had raised up difficulties to train Jacob. God had wrestled with Jacob not as an enemy but as a father.

And to what end? To the end that Jacob might become strong and mighty in wisdom and discernment. The goal, amazing and incredible as it sounds, was for Jacob to become strong enough to wrestle with the Angel of Yahweh and prevail.

God does not want slaves; nor does he want His people to be little children forever. He wants mature sons and daughters who can take their proper places at His right hand. Abraham had matured through patient faith to the point where he was welcomed as a prophet, a member of God's council, as one whom God desired to hear. Jacob had matured through wrestling faith to the point where he could wrestle with God and prevail. In both cases the development took a long time and involved patience and perseverance. The contrast is with Adam, Ham, Lot, and Esau, who were all impatient and never attained this high standing with God as a result.

It is instructive to notice how humble these two great men, Abraham and Jacob, were. When God gave Abraham the privilege of advising Him, Abraham did not speak to God as an equal. On the contrary, Abraham was most careful to give his advice with all humility, as God's junior partner, and as one who was but dust and ashes: "Now behold, I have ventured to speak to Yahweh, although I am dust and ashes" (Gen. 18:27). And again, "Oh may Yahweh not be angry, and I shall speak. . . .Now behold, I have undertaken to speak to Yahweh. . . .Oh may Yahweh not be angry, and I shall speak only this once" (Gen. 18:30-32). There is not the slightest trace of arrogance here. Abraham had been elevated to the high office of council member—God's junior partner—but he never forgot the infinite distance between himself and his Creator. This is true Christian humanism.

We see the same thing with Jacob. What did it mean to wrestle with God and prevail? Did it mean that Jacob could now dominate God? Never. It meant just the opposite. Jacob was wrestling for God's blessing: "I will not let you go unless you bless me" (Gen. 32:26). Jacob wrestled to be in *submission* to God. He fought to be in the kingdom of God, under the rule of the King (cf. Lk. 16:16). The man who seeks to be submitted to God is the man who wrestles with God and prevails. This is true Christian humanism.

We see that the man God chooses to make His covenantal

partner is precisely the man most aware of his helplessness and unworthiness before God. At the same time, looking back at Adam, we see that the false humanist who tries to seize equality with God is precisely the man with the highest opinion of himself.

Jacob's Rewards

Jacob received two special rewards. The first was to be named "Israel." Earlier we explained this name as meaning "One Who Wrestles With God." This name can just as easily mean "God's Wrestler," meaning the man who is God's champion on the earth. It can also mean "God Wrestles," meaning that this is a man with whom God wrestles, who is accounted worthy of God's special attention. We are not to try and choose which of these three meanings is correct, for they are all correct. All three are accurate descriptions of any person who is part of the true Israel of God (Gal. 6:16).

A bruised thigh was Jacob's other reward, so that for the rest of his life he limped (Gen. 32:25–32). His limp was not a sign of his defeat but of his victory. We get a snapshot of this in Genesis 32:31, "Now the sun rose upon him just as he crossed over Penuel, and he was limping on his thigh." As Jacob crossed joyously over the river into the promised land, we see the sun rise behind him. The rising of the sun is a sign of victory and might (Judg. 5:31; 8:4, 13; Rev. 1:16). Jacob could be assured of victory because of his limp.

This was because Jacob understood the prophecy of Genesis 3:15, that the Messiah would bruise the serpent on the head, while the serpent would bruise the Messiah, and all God's people, in the heel. Which would you rather have, a bruised heel or a crushed head?

The Church always limps, and this is because she always has the bruised heel. There are always embarrassments. There is always infighting. There are always inadequate responses. There are always problems. This can be very discouraging, especially when we look at the well-ordered troops in Satan's army. They don't seem to limp. They stride forward boldly and confidently, carrying out their plans in concert and unity—or so it appears.

Yet from the perspective of eternity things look radically different. The head of the enemy, Satan, is crushed. The enemy's army may have good feet and be able to march, but it has no unifying philosophy, no head. It also has no patience and no perseverance. When history is over, what looked like the enemy's well-coordinated effort will be shown to have been a rout, for no army can endure without a head.

And the Church? Her Head is alive! He coordinates His limping kingdom by His Spirit. What looks like chaos to us, as the Church limps in circles, is from the perspective of eternity a beautiful dance, outwardly spiralling—a dance that will eventually draw all the universe into itself. The limping Church is sure to win eventually because a headless army of opposition cannot endure.

Jacob's limp, though painful, was his reminder that he had wrestled with God and prevailed. It was the sign of his victory, of his eternal security as a member of God's kingdom, and of the eventual victory of God's holy kingdom.

Jacob's limp was also his reminder that as God's Champion he would often prevail not by means of a direct assault but by yielding to his enemies. Like Isaac in Philistia, he would often move on and dig another well when he encountered opposition. When compelled to go one mile, he would go a second mile. He would pay his taxes and submit to human authority, even when that authority was oppressive. He would take up a shame-filled cross and carry it in humility. Like a skillful wrestler, he would be willing to fall to the ground in order to get a better grip upon his opponent. In this way, he would eventually prevail.

Conclusion

What incredible privileges these men had! To be a member of God's council and to be taken with utmost gravity and seriousness by the Lord Himself! To wrestle with God and prevail! It is almost beyond imagining.

It took ninety-nine years for Abraham to mature to the point of being made a prophet, and it took ninety-seven years for Jacob to prevail with God. Yet, great as their privileges were, there was more to come. The privileges expanded over time. At first the sun was rising and the Angel of Yahweh refused to be seen (Gen. 32:26). Night comes before day in Scripture (Gen. 1, "evening and morning"), and God was not ready to be seen by men. Then Jacob asked His Name, and God refused to give it. Later Moses came to a higher privilege: God refused to show Moses His face or give him His Name (Exod. 3:13–15; 33:20), but God did permit Moses to see His glory and His "backside," the "backside" of His Name (Exod. 33:18–23; 34:5–7). Thus Moses became the greatest of the former day prophets, a man with whom God counselled (Num. 12:6–8).

The greatest of the prophets, however, was John the Forerunner (Mt. 11:11). Why? Because he saw the Angel of Yahweh, Jesus Christ, face to face, and heard His name. Yet all Christians, even the least in the kingdom, are greater than John, because in Christ we are seated in the heavenlies at the right hand of the Father and have access to the Council in prayer at any time (Eph. 2:6; Heb. 9:7; 10:19–22; 2 Cor. 3:18).

Do we appreciate the greatness of our privilege, or do we take it for granted? The lives of Abraham and Jacob teach us that if we want to enter into the fullness of participating in our incredible privilege, we must learn patient faith and submissive, wrestling faith. We can do so, confident that the limp of victory in Christ will mature into the dance of eternity.

10 FAITH AND SERVICE
The Story of Joseph

The Bible teaches us that while rulers among the pagans love to lord it over their subjects, Christians achieve power through *service* (Mk. 10:42–45). Power flows to those who accept responsibility, and there is no finer illustration of this principle and its effects than the history of Joseph.

The first appearance of Joseph in the Bible is as a righteous judge, the right-hand man of his father (Gen. 37:2-3). Like his father Jacob, Joseph was a man of books and ledgers, not a "macho man" of the hunt like his uncle Esau. Because Joseph was honest and shrewd, his father had him evaluate the activities of his brethren and bring home a report on them (Gen. 37:2, 14).

To reward his faithful service, Joseph's father made for him a splendid *vestment.* Placing it on Joseph, Jacob invested his son with his own authority. From that day on Joseph was in some respects second only to Jacob in the house. When his envious brothers attacked Joseph, the first thing they did was tear off his garment of glory and beauty (Gen. 37:3, 23). The power of envy is such that they sought to kill him and were only kept from it with difficulty (Gen. 37:21–28).

Service for Potiphar

Joseph was sold to a household in Egypt. The first phase of his service was in the house of Potiphar (Gen. 39:1–7). Joseph did not see his enslavement as a cause for resentment or bitterness. We do not see him throwing spanners into the works or sand into the machinery. He was willing to limp, like Israel his father, for God. Joseph served dutifully and well. As a result,

Potiphar gladly entrusted more and more of the household responsibilities to Joseph. Soon Joseph was in charge of everything, and Potiphar "did not concern himself with anything except the food he ate" (Gen. 39:6). Though Joseph had the name of slave, he was actually exercising considerable dominion. Indeed, since Potiphar was the captain of Pharaoh's personal bodyguard, it is likely that Joseph also had some influence at court and was known to important and influential people.

The point was not lost on the wife of Potiphar. She knew who the real power in the house was. Like the camp followers of all ages, the wife of Potiphar tried to involve herself with the man of power, but Joseph refused her advances (Gen. 39:7–12). Though a servant of men, he was first and foremost the servant of God. The fact that Joseph was stripped of his robe by Potiphar's wife is symbolic of his loss of power in Potiphar's house because of her actions.[1] At this point in the story it appears that the benefits Joseph was gaining from faithful service have been compromised by his virtuous adherence to the law of God. But the story is not yet over.

From Prison to Power

The vengeance of the wife of Potiphar landed Joseph in prison.[2] There again he ruled in life (Gen. 39:20–23). Because

---

[1] The word *garment* occurs six times in Genesis 39:12–18. The word *hand,* speaking of power, occurs nine times in the chapter. Six times it is said that Joseph's masters gave things into his *hand* (vv. 3, 4, 6, 8, 22, 23). Twice we are told that Joseph's *garment* was taken by the wife's *hand* (vv. 12, 13). Her power stripped Joseph of his.

[2] Why didn't Potiphar kill Joseph? We should expect a slave who attempts to rape the wife of his master to be tortured and put to death! It is clear that Potiphar did not believe his wife's story. He trusted Joseph more than he did her.

According to Genesis 39:14, this woman had her own household, and thus she was of an important family herself. Her accusations could not simply be ignored. It was her word against Joseph's, and obviously the word of a foreign slave counted for little before the law. But, according to the same verse and also 39:17, the wife blamed Potiphar, not Joseph, for of his responsible and effective service to those in charge, Joseph was soon put in charge of the entire prison. He had the name of prisoner, but he was exercising dominion. From that position, he could do much good. By being a slave *par excellence,* Joseph was acquiring mastery over the house.

We shall consider Joseph's experience in prison and his elevation to Pharaoh's right hand in chapter 11. For now let us consider that the story of Joseph shows us the means whereby he was enabled to rule in the midst of enslavement: he understood and applied the Word of God, which came to him in the form of family traditions and dreams and which comes to us in the form of Holy Scripture. He understood the principles by which God rules the world, and because he was able to apply them accurately to the situations in which he found himself, Joseph proved of inestimable value to every master who employed him. In time he was exalted to second-in-command over all Egypt (Gen. 41:40ff.). Again he was invested with authority, this time with the robe of Pharaoh (Gen. 41:42). As Joseph later put it, he came to be a father to Pharaoh (Gen. 45:8)—in other words, the power behind the throne. Pharaoh made no decisions without consulting Joseph. From this position of authority Joseph was able to feed the entire world (Gen. 41:57).

There are lessons here for oppressed Christians wherever in the world they may be. It is all too easy to yield to sinful temptation and seek to obstruct the designs of heathen masters by

the incident, and Potiphar's anger burned when she made that accusation (v. 19). Clearly Potiphar's anger was against his wife, not against Joseph.

It should also be noticed that the overseer of the prison wherein Joseph was incarcerated was none other than Potiphar himself (Gen. 39:1 with 40:3 and 39:20). Potiphar figured he could still make good use of Joseph in prison by letting him run things there. So, instead of putting him to death, Potiphar "punished" Joseph by casting him into prison and putting him in charge of everything.

We can also note that since this was the prison into which royal officials such as the cupbearer and baker were placed, it was a fairly decent place. It was not a pleasant place, but it was hardly a dungeon either. Here also we see Potiphar caring for Joseph as best he was able.

demonstrating half-hearted obedience or active meddling. The
story of Joseph tells us that the road to victory, dominion, and
mastery is through service, the humble service of a slave.
Through service and suffering God purges and destroys ind-
welling sin in the believer, builds character in him, and fits him
for the mastery of some portion of the world. As the lazy wicked
see that they can trust the hard-working righteous to keep the
machinery running, they will be inclined to turn it over to them.

Redeeming the Brethren

Simply acquiring dominion is not a worthy goal in itself.
Dominion can be used for selfish ends. The reason God gives
power to Christians is so that they can help others, so they can
restore and glorify His world. Joseph, of course, was able to help
feed the world. He was also enabled to deliver his brethren from
their bondage to sin and death.

Eye for eye and tooth for tooth—it is a fitting reward for those
who unjustly sell others into slavery that they themselves be
enslaved. When there was a famine in all the world Joseph's
brothers came to Egypt to buy bread. They were required to
approach the most important man in Egypt next to Pharaoh—
Joseph—but they did not recognize him. Joseph accused them
of being spies. They thought he meant that they had come to
spy out the land of Egypt, and he let them worry about this.
But he really meant that they were by nature spies, for they had
spied Joseph from afar and then determined to kill him (Gen.
37:18; 42:8–16).

Joseph threw them into prison (Gen. 42:17), and their
thoughts turned, as those of the guilty often do, to the preeminent wrong they had committed years before (Gen. 42:21f.).
Fear of judgment in general brought their specific guilt to mind.

Joseph cast them into prison for three days, saying that this
was Pharaoh's will (Gen. 42:15–17). Then he released them,

saying that this was God's will (v. 18). Years before, when he was in prison, Joseph had appealed to Pharaoh, and nothing happened (Gen. 40:14–15, 23). Three years later, when Joseph stood before Pharaoh, he did not appeal to Pharaoh but instead proclaimed the truth of God (Gen. 41:1, 16, 25, 28, 32). Joseph had learned that while it is not wrong to "appeal to Caesar," as Paul did, our ultimate appeal must be to God and not to man. Now he put his brothers through a similar experience, to teach them the same lesson. They had come to Egypt for bread. That was not wrong in itself. But they were not trusting God as they should, and ultimately it is only God who can "give us this day our daily bread."

On their way home the brothers found all their money in their sacks. They knew that "the Egyptian man" had returned it to them. By refusing to accept their money, Joseph put them in his debt. This increased their worry, for they knew that the borrower is slave to the lender (Prov. 22:7).

A year later, the brothers came back to Egypt to buy more bread. Because Joseph had insisted on it they brought their youngest brother, Benjamin, with them. Joseph intended to use Benjamin to test his brothers, to give them an opportunity to repent of their sins. The brothers had been envious when Jacob gave special honor to Joseph, and they had sought to kill him. Now, Joseph went out of his way to show special honor to Benjamin to see how they would react (Gen. 43:34).

As the brothers returned to Canaan from this second visit to Egypt, Joseph arranged for them to "steal" his silver cup. The brothers, believing themselves innocent, vowed to become slaves if the guilty party were found among them, while the actual thief would be put to death (Gen. 44:9). The penalty for theft, however, is not death but enslavement (Exod. 22:3), and so Joseph required the enslavement of the guilty party only (Gen. 44:17). It turned out to be Benjamin who had been framed as the thief—and not just a thief. The silver cup was specifically called a cup used for *divination,* that is, foretelling the future (Gen. 44:4–6). To all appearances, Benjamin was trying to set himself up as a prophet, a dreamer. He had accepted special privileges over his older brothers, and he had apparently stolen a device to help him tell the future.

Years before, when the brothers attacked Joseph and sold him into slavery, they had hated two things about him. They had hated his special privileges, symbolized by the garment they stripped off him. And they hated his dreams, his foretelling of the future. As they plotted to kill him, "they said to one another, 'Behold, the master of dreams comes!'" (Gen. 37:18–19). Now it seemed that Benjamin was following in the footsteps of his brother. How would his half-brothers respond? Perhaps they would let Benjamin take the penalty and escape scot-free themselves. That is what they would have done with Joseph.

Something different happened this time, however. Judah, who had been the ringleader in the attack on Joseph (Gen. 37:26), now stepped forward and begged to be enslaved in Benjamin's stead (Gen. 44:33). This was the attitude of repentance and self-sacrifice that Joseph had been looking for. Joseph made himself known to his brothers, and in giving them changes of garments (Gen. 45:22), he elevated them to dominical offices of some sort (again, through investiture).

Eye for eye and tooth for tooth, the brothers deserved punishment. But grace gives "much more" than law, and after having given them a taste of suffering, Joseph acted to redeem them from bondage and enthrone them with him as lords of the world.

Whom to Trust

There is an additional dimension to the fact that Joseph's silver cup is called a "cup of divination" (Gen. 44:5). While pretending to be an Egyptian lord, Joseph said to the brothers,

"Do you not know that such a man as I can indeed practice divination?" (Gen. 44:15).

Divination is a demonic practice and forbidden to the children of God (Lev. 19:26; Num. 23:23). Clearly Joseph did not in fact practice divination. The cup is initially referred to simply as "my cup, the silver cup" (Gen. 44:2). Yet Joseph told his steward to claim that it was a cup of divination, and Joseph also carried on this pretense. Why?

The answer lies in the fact that divination had been part of the Egyptian occultist-demonic religion, and the covenant people were looking for food from Egypt (and her gods) rather than to Yahweh.[3] Instead of looking to their God, Yahweh, for deliverance, they were looking to an apparently heathen Egyptian vizier. In the crisis their thoughts did not turn to Yahweh for help, but to the statist power that overshadowed their land. Thus, Joseph asked them, "Do you not know that *such a man as I* can indeed practice divination?" That is, did you not realize that in a culture such as Egypt, a person in my position would certainly be a diviner?[4] In fact Joseph was a diviner of sorts. He had been given prophetic dreams by God in his youth (Gen. 37:5–11). The brothers had rejected these true divinations sent by Yahweh and instead turned to the apparently idolatrous divination of Egypt.

To heighten their awareness of their sin, Joseph and the Egyptians refused to eat with the Hebrews at the same table (Gen. 43:32). Eating bread with the Hebrews was "an abomination" to the Egyptians. The term "abomination" refers to a religious and sacramental distinction, and so setting up the two

[3]Oddly enough, just a few years earlier Pharaoh had become disgusted with Egyptian food and begun looking for something better, as we shall see in our next chapter.

[4]Joseph had shown them "mysterious" knowledge when he arranged them at the table in their order of birth (Gen. 43:33). Since the brothers were from four different mothers and, except for Benjamin, were roughly the same age, it would have been impossible to rank them by age unless one actually knew how old each was in relation to the rest. Joseph had this knowledge from his youth, of course, but the brothers had no way of knowing that at this point.

tables indicated a religious separation. The brothers assumed
that the Egyptians were idolaters and that this was the reason
they would not eat with those who worshipped Yahweh. The
irony is that Joseph and the Egyptians were in fact converted
worshipers of the true God, and the reason they would not eat
with the brothers was because the *brothers* were committing
idolatry!

Joseph's actions thus constituted a dramatic parable designed
to show them that if they looked to Egypt for salvation, they
would be looking to Egypt's gods as well. And if they looked to
Egypt for salvation, they would become slaves of Egypt. This is
according to the biblical principle that *the one who saves is the
one who rules* (Judg. 8:22; Lk. 1:71, 74, 75; Exod. 20:2ff.). What
rescued them from bondage to Egypt at this point was the fact
that Joseph was, contrary to appearances, not an Egyptian idola-
ter but a covenant worshiper of the only true and living God.

Restoring Community

The history of the patriarchs in Genesis, from Abram forward, moves from family to nation. The rule of a father over
one or two sons is one thing, but the rule of a man over a dozen
sons and their own communities of people is quite another. The
Hebrews were becoming a nation, and a nation requires a more
extensive kind of government than a mere family or clan. A
nation requires an objective written law, which God would give
them through Moses. It also requires a system of judges ending
in a supreme judge who is not merely the head of one family.
With Joseph, and later with Moses, we see the appearance of
such a supreme judge.[5]

---

[5] The eventual appearance of a king is prophesied at the time Benjamin is born (Gen.
35:11,18). Benjamin means "Son of the Right Hand," a name that associates him with
kingship, as the king sits at the father's right hand. The first king of Israel, Saul, came
from Benjamin. But it is Judah who, after sinning, reveals what a true king is like as he
offers to give his life for Benjamin (Gen. 43:9; 44:18–34; 49:10). David and Jesus came
from Judah.

In Genesis 36, we see how the individual man Esau became the nation of Edom. The same thing was happening to the individual man Jacob. The great emphasis on Jacob's flocks in Genesis 30 parallels the birth of his many sons in Genesis 29 and 30.[6] None of Jacob's sheep were pure white, and none of his goats were pure black, which is a symbol of the fact that in this world none of God's people are pure sheep, and none of His enemies are yet totally wicked. Jacob's flocks were a picture of the nation of Israel.

Jacob's numerous sons proved hard to govern. We see them acting vilely in Genesis 34, where they massacred a city of newly-circumcised "brothers" to avenge a wrong that these people had openly repented of. We see them acting to "murder" Joseph. Jacob strongly suspected his sons of perfidy and refused to be comforted by them (Gen. 37:35). When the famine begins we find that Jacob's sons are fighting among themselves: Genesis 42:1 literally reads, "Why are you glaring at [or, arguing with] one another?" When the brothers return from Egypt, Jacob virtually disowns them, temporarily at least (Gen. 42:36, which implies "I no longer have any sons"). Later, when the brothers need to return to Egypt to buy more grain, Jacob does not trust them to care for Benjamin (Gen. 43:1–14). This is a society torn apart by suspicion and strife.

Joseph's actions not only restore his brothers individually but also heal the society. The brothers are reconciled with him, with each other, and with their father Jacob. The story emphasizes death and life. Jacob says at the beginning, in Genesis 42:2, "Behold, I have heard that there is grain in Egypt; go down there and buy for us from there, so that we may *live and not die*." Joseph uses the same life and death language when he restores the

---

[6] Genesis 27:9 is only the tenth mention of "flock" in Genesis. In the ensuing story, Jacob is associated with a flock 38 times. Totalling all the words for sheep, goat, he-goat, ewe, lamb, flock, etc., we find 55 occurrences in the story of Jacob (Gen. 25:19-35:29). In the Joseph narrative (Gen. 37–50), "flock" occurs 15 times. Thus, Jacob's sons and daughters are clearly to be linked with flocks.

brothers from their first experience of prison (Gen. 42:18–20). When the brothers seek to return to Egypt, Judah says, "We will arise and go, that we may live and not die" (Gen. 43:8).

The brothers bring back life-giving bread from their first trip to Egypt, but Jacob only experiences more death: "You have bereaved me of my sons. Joseph is no more, and Simeon is no more, and you would take Benjamin" (Gen. 42:36). Then Reuben foolishly offers to let Jacob put his own two sons to death as a surety for Benjamin, an act that would only add to Jacob's grief (Gen. 42:37). When Jacob finally sends his sons back to Egypt again, he says, "As for me, if I am bereaved of my children, I am bereaved" (Gen. 43:14).

What brought Jacob back to life was the gospel, the "good news" that Joseph lived and reigned in Egypt; that Joseph, who had been "dead," was now alive and enthroned. When the brothers "told him all the words of Joseph that he had spoken to them, and when he saw the wagons that Joseph had sent to carry him, *the spirit of their father Jacob revived*" (Gen. 45:27). The good news snapped Jacob out of the lethargy and horror in which he had been living for years.

Though He sometimes takes them through "the valley of the shadow of death," God will in time revive the hearts of those who cling to Him. Tough times don't last forever, but faithful people do. This is true not only of individuals, like Jacob, but of communities as well. The fledgling nation of Israel needed to pass through death and judgment before coming to resurrection and restoration as a community. This should encourage us, for it means that God never lets His people go. Whatever we as individuals or as communities may pass through, it is only part of God's good plan for us.

Conclusion

First, a cautionary note. Joseph's manipulation of his brothers, like Rebekah's "wise woman" manipulation of Isaac, is a
model of great wisdom. It is not something Christians should
try to copy unless they are very wise and insightful. Joseph's
manipulation of his brethren should be seen as the way Jesus
manipulates our lives. Just as the circumstances of their lives
showed the brothers their sins, so we must be alert to ironies
that God brings about in our own lives, and we must change
our ways if necessary.

The road to true dominion is through service. Paul counselled all employees and subordinates: "Servants, be obedient
to those who are your masters according to the flesh, with fear
and trembling, in the sincerity of your heart, as to Christ; not
by way of mere eye-service, as men-pleasers, but as slaves of
Christ, doing the will of God from the heart. With good will
render service, as to the Lord, and not to men, knowing that
whatever good thing each one does, this he will receive back
from the Lord, whether slave or free" (Eph. 6:5–8).

The road to dominion through service is often difficult.
Doubtless there were many days when Joseph had to pray for
God to give him a gracious and obedient spirit because he simply did not want to work. Yet he found God was gracious to
help him do what had been set before him.

The road to dominion through service is not always a straight
one. Joseph was faithful to his father, and it landed him in slavery. He was faithful to Potiphar, and it landed him in prison.
There were ups and downs. Yet in the end he was placed over
the entire world of that day. The story of Joseph is an encouragement to Christians who labor hard only to have their works
shattered by the envious and wicked who are all too frequently
found in the Church herself. The story of Joseph tells us to learn

from our experiences and pick up and move on in faithful service to whatever vineyard we have been given, even if the new one is smaller than the old.

The road to dominion must never be understood in a pagan sense of sheer triumph and overlording. Joseph was given dominion precisely so that he could become a more effective servant. He moved from serving his father to serving Potiphar, from serving Potiphar in his household to serving Potiphar in prison, from serving in prison to serving all the people of the world, and from serving all people in general to having the wisdom to restore his own family. When Joseph was raised from prison he was no longer severely oppressed, but he never ceased being a servant. The Christian hope is not to escape service, but to escape bondage to sin, death, and tyranny. Humble service and dominion can never be separated.

11 FAITH AND THE WORLD
The Story of Pharaoh

Pharaoh was hungry. Pharaoh was dissatisfied. The bread that was on his table tasted stale. It was just not as good as it used to be. Bad bread, day after day, was not what the emperor of the known world expected to be served.

The wine was no better. It was old. It tasted like vinegar. Pharaoh was frustrated.

He called for his chief baker and for his chief butler (or cupbearer). "Taste this stuff," he said.

They did. "We don't see any problem with it. It is the same as we've always served," they replied.

"Well," said Pharaoh, "it doesn't taste very good to me any longer. Improve the recipe. I'll give each of you a week to find something better to serve me. If not, I'll make you pay."

Bread and wine together are the food of kings. After Abram defeated Chedorlaomer and showed that he was the true heir of the promised land, Melchizedek brought out bread and wine to honor him (Gen. 14:18). But there was more to being chief baker and chief butler than merely serving bread and wine to the king. They were both high officials in Pharaoh's court.[1]

The chief baker and cupbearer were among Pharaoh's most trusted officials, possibly the most trusted of all. Kings live in danger of poisoning. Those entrusted with his food had to be extremely reliable and loyal. Such men inevitably have the ear

[1] "The titles 'chief of the butlers' and 'chief of the bakers' (Gen. 40:2) are those of palace officials mentioned in Egyptian writings;" G. E. Wright and F. V. Wilson, *The Westminster Historical Atlas to the Bible* (Philadelphia: Westminster Press, 1956), p. 28b. K. A. Kitchen remarks concerning the cupbearer, "The officials (often foreigners) became in many cases confidants and favorites of the king and wielded political influence;" *The New Bible Dictionary* (Grand Rapids: Eerdmans, 1972), p. 283.

of the king. But more than that, being so trustworthy, they also often have larger responsibilities in the kingdom.

Possibly the chief baker was in charge of all the food in the kingdom. He would oversee the crops and planting in the entire land of Egypt, ensuring that every person got his proper share and that Pharaoh got his proper share as well. If so, he was Secretary of Agriculture.[2] Similarly, the chief cupbearer was very close to the king. Divination was practiced using the cup (Gen. 44:5), and the chief cupbearer is counted among the "wise men and magicians" of Genesis 41:8–9. (Nehemiah held a position of similar importance; Neh. 1:11; 2:1.)

Both of these men were high in the councils of the Pharaoh. We don't really know why Pharaoh was offended at his chief baker and chief cupbearer. What is clear is that he was unhappy with the old administration, so unhappy that he threw both men into prison to think about it.

There they encountered Joseph, and there each had a dream (Gen. 40). The cupbearer dreamed of a vine with three branches and clusters of ripe grapes. He saw himself squeezing the grapes into Pharaoh's cup and serving him. Joseph told him that the three branches were three days and that in three days the cupbearer would be elevated to his former position and once

---

[2] Possibly the chief baker had a religious function. The Egyptians were apparently unique in the ancient world in learning that sourdough contains yeast, and they were the first people to make yeast-raised bread. As such, they were "the envy of the ancient world." This statement by Trager implies that the Egyptians kept the secret to themselves. James G. Trager, Jr., *The Enriched, Fortified, Concentrated, Country-Fresh, Lip-Smacking, Finger-Licking, International, Unexpurgated Foodbook* (New York: Grossman Pub., 1970), p. 15f. (Despite its title, this book is a serious history of food.) It is easy to imagine that yeast baking was a jealously guarded procedure and that the chief baker had an especially important, and priestly, function in Egypt because of it. If this be true—that Egyptian leaven was pure yeast and a secret guarded by priests—it adds another dimension to the biblical concept of "the leaven of Egypt."

The cupbearer was one of Pharaoh's wise men, as we see in Genesis 41. If the baker was a priest of sorts, then Genesis 40 anticipates the need for better priests and wise men, which is a theme in Genesis 41.

again serve Pharaoh. The interpretation was not overly difficult, because Joseph, like everyone in Egypt, knew that
Pharaoh's birthday was coming in three days. Once the "three
branches" were understood, the rest was easy.

The baker also had a dream. He dreamed of three baskets of
choice baked goods on his head, the kind Pharaoh favored.[3]
Once again the three baskets obviously were three days. But the
baker did not see himself serving Pharaoh. Birds were eating
the food out of the basket. The baker might not have understood the dire nature of his dream, but Joseph did. Joseph knew
that when God had made a covenant with his forefather Abram,
He had caused Abram to kill animals and divide them in half,
making a path. God's Spirit had moved between these divided
animals, symbolically restoring them and bringing them back
to life.[4] To be torn in half and devoured by birds and beasts is
what the Bible means by the "curse of the covenant."[5] Abram
had driven away the birds when they came to eat the carcasses
(Gen. 15:11). The birds eating the bread prepared by the baker,
and in particular eating it off of his head,[6] indicated that he was
about to be killed and devoured by the birds. It was the curse.

Pharaoh's birthday arrived three days later. You don't have a
birthday feast without good bread and wine—especially if you're
the Pharaoh—so something had to be done about the chief
baker and the chief cupbearer. Pharaoh decided, for reasons we

---

[3] "Egypt's virtuosity at bread making came not only from using yeast to make bread rise,
but also from using and blending various kinds of cereal grains to make breads of differing
degrees of fineness or coarseness. And while the dough was not always embellished, the
pharaoh's bakers as early as 4000 B.C. were mixing their best bread dough with honey, sweet
herbs, almonds, fruits, and spices which included saffron and cinnamon." *Ibid.,* p. 16. We
must question the date of 4000 B.C., because that predates the flood.

[4] The divided animals represented Abram's estrangement from the land, which is the
concern of his prayer in Genesis 15. Both man and animals are made from soil, so animals
are an appropriate symbol for both sides of the conflict. God's promise was that Abram would
be joined to the land through death and resurrection.

[5] See O. Palmer Robertson, *The Christ of the Covenants* (Grand Rapids: Baker, 1980),
pp. 128.

[6] The head wound is the curse of death (Gen. 3:15).

are not told, to restore the cupbearer, and replace the baker.
Pharaoh was still unhappy though. What he was searching
for had not come. There was no improvement on the old ways,
and the old ways were stale. Was there no better bread? Was there
no better wine? Was there nowhere in the land a man wise
enough to administer the kingdom?

Pharaoh's Nightmares

It was God who had made Pharaoh dissatisfied. God had
made Pharaoh want something better. And after precisely two
years, God sent two nightmares to Pharaoh on his birthday in
the night, nightmares that would completely shatter his humanistic worldview.

Pharaoh dreamed that he was standing by the Nile, and *out
of the Nile* came seven fat cows. Then seven gaunt cows came
out of the Nile and ate up the seven fat cows. This dream woke
Pharaoh up, but he eventually got back to sleep, only to have a
second dream. This time he saw seven plump ears of grain on
a single stalk. Soon seven thin ears, scorched by a wind *from the
Sun's rising*, grew up and devoured the seven plump ears. Again
this nightmare woke Pharaoh. He remained troubled until
morning (Gen. 41:1–8).

Pharaoh realized that these were no ordinary dreams but
visions. He called for his *priests to interpret* the dream, and his
wise men to advise him what to do based on the dreams' meaning. None was able to help him. At this point the chief cupbearer,
one of the wise men, spoke up and told Pharaoh about Joseph.
Joseph was immediately summoned and brought before Pharaoh. Upon hearing the dreams Joseph explained that the two
dreams were a double witness to one prophecy. There would
be seven years of plenty followed by seven years of famine.
Having interpreted the message from God as a true *priest*, Joseph went on to show himself a *wise man* by advising Pharaoh

to gather food during the seven fat years as a reserve for the seven years of famine.

These events shattered Pharaoh's worldview in two ways. First, the very fact of the vision itself was a refutation of the wisdom of the empire. Egyptian ways of knowing were called into question.[7] The priests and wise men were unable to interpret the visions. This was strange because one of the primary duties of pagan priests was to interpret oracles and dreams. This dream, however, had come from God Most High, and the priests of Egypt were totally incompetent to deal with it. The Egyptian worldview, like modern uniformitarian humanism, was based on the presupposition of an *eternal, unchanging regularity of natural causes*. Each year the Nile flooded. Every year the sun shone down and the crops grew. Application of proper techniques would ensure the same good crop year after year. If you understand *natural law* and manipulate the world in terms of it, you will succeed. The invasion of the supernatural Word of God, with its message of a coming supernatural Divine intervention in history, was something the closed worldview of the Egyptian sages could not handle.

Second, the *content* of the dream was a direct attack upon Egyptian philosophy. We emphasized earlier that the cows came out of the Nile. In Egyptian theology, the Nile was seen as the source of life. (This is why the first of the Mosaic plagues was against the Nile.) There is no rain in Egypt, and there is only one river. Thus, in a sense, all life does come out of the Nile as a result of its annual flooding. Brueggemann comments that "the Nile River is not only a geographical referent. It is also an expression of the imperial power of fertility. It is administration of the Nile that permits the king to generate and

---

[7] For some of these insights I am indebted to Walter Brueggemann, *Genesis* (Atlanta: John Knox Press, 1982), pp. 326.

guarantee life. The failure of the Nile and its life system means that the empire does not have in itself the power of life."[8]

The bad ears of grain came from the sun. The "east wind" of Genesis 41:6 comes from the place where the sun rises. The sun was the other principal god of Egypt (which is why the ninth of the Mosaic plagues was against the sun).

The Pharaoh and his bureaucracy were administrators of the Nile and of the sun. The king made sure that crops were properly planted and harvested, irrigation systems maintained, and so forth. Life came from the Nile and the sun, and the Pharaoh administered that life. Now came a pair of dreams that asserted something radically different. Life comes from God, said the dreams, and Pharaoh has no control over it. God can send fat cows out of the Nile, but He can also send gaunt cows. God can send good grain growing in sunlight, but He can also send bad grain. God Most High, whose priests are the Hebrews, is in charge, not Pharaoh.

The Word of God directly challenged Egyptian humanism. How would Pharaoh respond?

Pharaoh's Response

In the book of Genesis we have seen Cain go out and build a city, only to have it destroyed in the flood. Immediately after the flood, men attempted another humanistic civilization in the Tower of Babel, though God thwarted their plans. Beginning with the history of Abraham, we encounter Egypt. Egypt is the most fundamental expression of Cainite imperialism in the books of Genesis and Exodus.

God has two ways of dealing with Cainite tyranny. One is to judge the tyrant and deliver His people. We see this in Genesis 12, where Abram and Sarai are delivered from Pharaoh's attacks,

[8] *Ibid.,* p. 327.

and we see it in the story of the Mosaic exodus in the early chapters of the book of Exodus. The other way God deals with Cainite culture is to confront it and convert it. Abimelech is converted in Genesis 20, and his successor is converted in Genesis 26; both chose to ally with God's people and bless them. (Abimelech and his Philistines were Egyptians; Gen. 10:13–14.) In Daniel 4 Nebuchadnezzar is converted. That is also what happened to Pharaoh.

The text of Genesis shows that Pharaoh and the Egyptians were converted to the service of the true God, but for some reason this is hard to believe. Let us consider a number of arguments for it.

First, if Pharaoh had not been open to God's Word, he would have rejected it. Genesis 41:37 says that Joseph's "word was good in the sight of Pharaoh and in the sight of all his servants." This is not the way unconverted people respond when the Word of God attacks their whole worldview!

Second, Pharaoh's own confession of the faith comes in verse 38, "Can we find a man like this, in whom is the Spirit of God?" Some modern translators are certain that Pharaoh could not have said this. The New International Version gives a footnote "or, spirit of the gods." The New American Standard Bible is even more blatant, with "in whom is a divine spirit." That is not what the text says. Pharaoh recognized Who was speaking through Joseph.

Third, Pharaoh elevated Joseph to second in command over all Egypt, precisely because of his faith: "Since God has informed you of all this, there is no one so discerning and wise as you are. You shall be over all my house" (vv. 39–40). Pharaoh recognized that Joseph's wisdom came from his relationship to the Word of God, the Second Person of the Trinity, who would be born into the world as Jesus Christ.

Fourth, note that Joseph married Asenath, the daughter of Potiphera, priest of Heliopolis (Gen. 41:45). Would the man who refused Potiphar's wife marry a heathen, knowing how mixed marriages had corrupted the world before the flood, and how Esau's marriages had vexed the covenant community? No. We are driven to consider that these people had become converted to the true faith. (Compare with Gen. 43:23.)

Fifth, these events fulfill the Abrahamic covenant, "I will bless those who bless you, and the one who curses you I will curse" (Gen. 12:3). When the Pharaoh of Genesis 12 had "cursed" Abram, God "cursed" him. Now a Pharaoh acts to bless Joseph and his family. This point is reiterated throughout the succeeding chapters. Pharaoh elevates Joseph over all Egypt. Pharaoh and his servants rejoice when Joseph's brothers are blessed (Gen. 45:16). Pharaoh orders that the very best of the land be given to Joseph's people (Gen. 45:17–20). In return, Jacob blesses Pharaoh (Gen. 47:7, 10). We probably should picture Pharaoh on his knees, receiving Jacob's blessing. Can we doubt that this was true conversion? Finally, when Jacob died, the Egyptians mourned for seventy days and went along for the funeral and burial (Gen. 50:3, 7). Through all of this, the only attitude we see is one of covenant loyalty and love for God's people on the part of the Egyptians.

Sixth, these events fulfill another aspect of the Abrahamic covenant: "You shall be the father of a multitude of nations" (Gen. 17:5). While this promise has a "literal" or physical fulfillment in the several nations that came from Abraham's loins, it has a more basic spiritual fulfillment in all those who convert to Abraham's faith. This is not some New Testament innovation: Joseph uses precisely this language in Genesis 45:8, saying "God has made me a father to Pharaoh." If Joseph had become Pharaoh's father, then Abraham was also his father. This indicates conversion, and it also indicates a fulfillment of the Abrahamic covenant.

Seventh, these events fulfill yet another aspect of the Abrahamic covenant: "In you all the families of the earth shall be blessed" (Gen. 12:3). Genesis 41 tells us that the famine was severe not only in Egypt but also in all the earth, so that the people of "all the earth came to Egypt to buy grain from Joseph" (v. 57). Since the Abrahamic covenant receives a preliminary fulfillment in the story of Joseph, and God's design in these events is to foreshadow the coming New Covenant and the blessing that would come to the whole world, it is even more obvious that a conversion of the nation of Egypt is in view.[9]

Finally, the New Testament comments on Pharaoh's conversion in a passage that is almost universally misinterpreted by New Testament commentators. I refer to Luke 4:16–30. Before looking at this let us review what happened when Joseph stood before the Gentile Pharaoh. Pharaoh marvelled at him, saying "Can we find a man like this?" Pharaoh also confessed that Joseph had the Spirit of God, saying "in him is the Spirit of God" (Gen. 41:38). Pharaoh blessed him and made him the ruler of all Egypt.

Now look at Luke 4. We see Jesus enter the synagogue and at the appointed time stand up to read. Jesus is given the scroll of Isaiah. He reads: "The Spirit of the Lord is upon Me, because He anointed Me to preach the gospel to the poor. He has sent Me to proclaim release to the captives, and recovery of sight to the blind, and to set free those who are downtrodden, to proclaim the favorable year of the Lord" (Lk. 4:18–19; Is. 61:1–2). Jesus states that this Scripture is being fulfilled that very day (Lk. 4:21).

Before considering the sequel, let us consider who these "poor, captive, blind, downtrodden" people are. Could it be that Jesus is referring to the Gentiles? In Romans 2 and 3, Paul argues that the Jews have all the advantages, and that the Gentiles are poor by comparison. Isaiah was not originally speaking of Gentiles, but is it possible that Jesus has them in mind?

---

[9] Of course, when we open the book of Exodus, we find that Egypt has fallen into apostasy, but that is later.

Look at what happens next: "And all were *speaking well* of
Him, and *wondering* at the *gracious* words which were falling
from His lips; and they were saying, 'Is this not the son of Joseph?'" (Lk. 4:22). Commentators take this as a reference to
Joseph the carpenter, but it is far more likely a reference to Joseph the patriarch. The "son of Joseph" was the Messiah. Like
Pharaoh, these people marvel at the words of this "son of Joseph." Like Pharaoh, they recognize, temporarily, that He has
the Spirit of God. The parallels are obvious and intense. The
Joseph spoken of here is the Joseph of Genesis.[10]

Jesus confirms our interpretation by what He does next. He
bluntly tells the Jews that the "poor, captive, blind, downtrodden" people are not the Jews but the Gentiles. He rejects the
thought of doing miracles for these Jews and reminds them that
Elijah was sent to heal a Gentile woman, not an Israelitess, and
that Elisha healed a Gentile leper, not Israelite lepers (Lk. 4:23–
27). Joseph had taken the gospel to the Gentiles. Could the Son
of Joseph do less?

The Jews were infuriated. They did not accept this greater
Joseph and sought to kill Him (Lk. 4:28–30). In this they were
like their ancestors. Joseph's brothers had tried to kill him while
the Gentile Pharaoh and his court accepted him.

Our purpose in making this excursion into Luke 4 has been
to provide further evidence that a true spiritual conversion of
Pharaoh and his Gentile Egyptians is in view in Genesis 41.
Jesus' allusions to this event help confirm our interpretation.

The book of Genesis opens with the Fall of man. God intervened to rescue humanity, eventually calling Abram to start up
a new world. In terms of God's promise and prophecy, all

[10] I would be willing to grant a possible *double entendre* in the text here, so that the Jews
referred to Joseph the carpenter, while Luke intends us also to think of Joseph the patriarch.
I think it far more likely, however, that when the Jews said, "Is this not the son of Joseph?"
they had the Messiah and the Joseph of Genesis in view. In Greek, the question implies an
expected answer of "yes."

nations would come to the faith of Abraham. This promise received a preliminary fulfillment in the conversion of Egypt at the end of the book of Genesis, and these events are a pledge that God will not rest until all nations are His.

Joseph's Service

The shift from the old pagan administration to the new godly one is indicated by the repeated use of the words "all" and "land/earth" (same Hebrew word) in verses 46–57 of Genesis 41. It is designed to indicate a total change: *"all* the *land* of Egypt (v. 46); . . . *all* the food (v. 48); . . . *all* my hardship, . . . *all* my father's house (v. 51); . . . *all* the *lands,* . . . *all* the *land* of Egypt (v. 54); . . . *all* the *land* of Egypt, . . . *all* the Egyptians (v. 55); . . . *all* the *land,* . . . *all* that was in the storehouses (v. 56); . . . *all* the *earth,* . . . *all* the *earth* (v. 57).

Joseph became the principal advisor to Pharaoh. We have noted that he became Pharaoh's "father." We should also notice the language of Genesis 41:40, "You shall be over my house, and according to your mouth all my people shall kiss; only in the throne will I be greater than you." *Kiss* here means *salute,* the homage rendered by an inferior to a superior. Joseph, in other words, would have the power to restructure the bureaucracy completely, setting up one and putting down another. Pharaoh also gave Joseph his signet ring (Gen. 41:42), which meant that any decision made by Joseph and sealed by the ring had all the authority of Pharaoh himself. Pharaoh said, "See, I have set you over all the land of Egypt" (Gen. 41:41).

Remember that Pharaoh had been looking for better bread and wine. With Joseph as his chief advisor, he has at last found them. When we see Joseph in charge of all the storehouses of Egyptian grain, we see him as the new chief baker (Gen. 41:46–57). We can also see Joseph as the new chief cupbearer, because of the special silver cup he carried (Gen. 44:2, 5, 12, 16-17).

Whether Joseph actually filled these offices or not, the way the story is written for us in Genesis points to his ministry as a replacement for both the baker and cupbearer. It was Joseph who brought new bread and wine to Egypt.

In Joseph's service to the world we see a picture of the ministry of the Church. It is the divine calling of the Church to speak the Word of God to men and offer them better bread and wine. The Church does not exist for her own sake but for the sake of the world. God wants a Christian world, and we have His promise that one day, some day, He will bring it to pass.

Conclusion

While he languished in prison, Joseph had no idea what was going on Pharaoh's heart. He did not realize that God the Holy Spirit was at work making Pharaoh dissatisfied. He did not know that one night God would bring His Word to Pharaoh, and Pharaoh would need someone to interpret it. He did not know that one day his suffering would be rewarded, and he would stand before the king of the earth.

This should encourage us. We pray for our rulers and those in authority over us, but we don't see them change. We have no way of knowing, however, what God may be doing. Our God is still the "God of Nightmares"! In our secular humanist society, Christians are often "in prison" in various ways. Yet God's Word is faithful, and the time will come when secular society will turn to God's people for help.

May we be ready for the day we stand before kings.

12   FAITH AND SLAVERY
The Story of the Egyptians

In Genesis 47 we have the account of Joseph's enslavement of the populace of Egypt. This passage has been a source of consternation for Christian thinkers throughout the ages. Was this sinful on Joseph's part? After all, nobody should ever be made a slave, should he? Should we say that the Egyptians, being heathen, deserved to be made slaves, and so it was proper for Joseph to enslave them? The purpose of this chapter is to explore the area afresh, to offer a third and hopefully more satisfying explanation.

The missing link in most interpretations of Genesis 47 is the conversion of Egypt. Since Egypt was at that time a converted people (as Nineveh became under Jonah later on), it seems that Joseph reduced fellow believers to bondage—which only seems to make the moral problem with his actions worse.

Jacob's blessing of Pharaoh must provide a canon governing our interpretation of the rest of Genesis 47. Joseph's enslavement was a blessing for the Egyptians; by implication it was part of the blessing Jacob bestowed on Pharaoh. Indeed, the Egyptians rejoiced at their enslavement, as we shall see.

Freedom and Security

To understand this we need to discuss the problem of freedom and security. Modern thinkers tend to pit these against each other. This is commonly seen in the political arena, where the contest is between the security of socialism and the freedom of libertarianism. As Christians we need to avoid being pulled into taking sides on such an issue. Security and freedom go together, and there cannot be one without the other.

Both security and freedom are vague concepts, but we have a general idea of what they mean, and generally speaking, freedom and security go hand in hand; they are not opposed to one another. If a man has no zone(s) of security in his life, and thus is totally "free," he in fact will not feel free at all. Instead, he will feel tremendous tension, a debilitating stress that will shorten his life, break his health, stifle his creativity, and prevent him from accomplishing what he might. This "freedom" is hardly worth celebrating.

On the other hand, if a man lives in a totalitarian society where he has no areas of freedom at all, he will not in fact feel secure. He will feel threatened by the very monolithic state that claims to give him security. This also will result in tension, loss of creativity, and so forth. This is hardly a "security" worth the name.

True security is the foundation of freedom. This is the beauty of any *feudal* system, and this is why Christianity has generally created some type of feudalism wherever it goes.[1]

Christianity puts the security factor primarily in the Church and secondarily in the family. It is the everlasting arms of the Triune God that provide our final security, but the womb of Mother Church should provide our fullest experience of this security in this present world. To a lesser degree, the family provides security, especially for the child. The family, however, is not a permanent institution but a transient one (Gen. 2:24). It cannot provide long-term, ongoing stability. The civil authority also provides some stability by securing us from harm at the hands of criminals and invaders. This, however, is more of a negative than a positive security.

The Church is supposed to provide the great psychological retreat for the psyche battered and bruised by sin, the world,

---

[1] On this see Rousas J. Rushdoony, *This Independent Republic* (Tyler: Thoburn Press, 1964).

the flesh, and the devil. The sabbath-security provided by the Church should give men a foundation for the freedom of action they manifest in the world. The tithe maintained by the Church should exist to support those who suffer financial disasters. The more developed a Christian society becomes, the more institutional presence the Church has, and the more fully capable she can become of providing security. While in our modern world the Church too often fails at this calling, it remains her duty, and her place in Christian social theory.

The arena of the marketplace is the primary area of freedom. The purpose of money and wealth is not primarily to provide security. When men come to trust in mammon for security they move into idolatry. Money and wealth provide freedom for action, for expansion, for dominion, for service. It is only in a secondary way that money provides security, and the security provided is not always psychologically effective. Many wealthy people are extremely insecure; indeed, they often seem to have more fears and worries than people much less well off. While money has a secondary value in providing security (a buried talent), it is primarily valuable for expansion and work (the talent put to work—Mt. 25:14–30).

Modern people pervert and actually reverse the zones of security and freedom. They want money, controlled by the state through taxation and regulation, to become the womb of society, providing security and comfort for men. They want religion, faith, and the institutional Church to be an area of freedom, of *angst*. The modernist rejects the "security" of an infallible Bible or a "cozy" Church.

Young Christians frequently do not understand how important is the zone of security and comfort provided by the institutional Church. As we grow older and life becomes more complicated, more distressing, and more grievous, the motherhood of the Church becomes more important to us. As the Church matures over time, she becomes more institutionalized and

provides more and more avenues of comfort and security for
her members—as well she should. Too many conservative
Christians tend to turn their Churches into centers of activism
and lose the ministry of comfort that should remain at her center.

We could keep talking about security and freedom for a long
time, but we have said enough to establish the point that they
are complimentary. This is an important point because *biblically speaking, slavery is not necessarily the opposite of freedom*. For
example, under the law if a man was sold into slavery briefly to
pay off a debt, he might come to find more true freedom as part
of the well-ordered household than he had enjoyed while out
in the world. He might ask to be adopted into the family of the
master by having his ear bored to the doorpost of the house
(Exod. 21).

Ultimately, the source of all freedom and security is God,
and thus the two cannot be in conflict. The more fully in covenant with God we are, the more free we are, and the more secure we are. As the Church has always taught, slavery to God is
the greatest freedom.

Freedom and security are not abstractions but relations and
experiences. When people are rightly related to God they experience both true freedom and true security. People may experience a false freedom and a false security apart from God, but
freedom and security are things *experienced.* If a serf in the
Middle Ages "felt" free under the protection of his lord, who
are we to say he was not "really" free? It is important to understand this, because it implies that freedom and security are both
highly relative matters, relative to various conditions of life.

The Egyptians did not perceive Joseph as an enslaver but as
a liberator. Their final statement to him was, "You have saved
our lives! Let us find favor in the sight of my lord, and we will
be Pharaoh's slaves" (Gen. 47:25). Even though they had been
"enslaved" they did not feel that they were slaves. They had been

delivered from the far more gruesome bondage of famine and death.

Biblically speaking, men cannot be absolutely free. They are always in bondage to someone: God or else the enemies of God. Men in bondage to God are truly free. Men in bondage to other men or in bondage to sin and the fear of death are not free. The question, then, is whether enslavement to Pharaoh was a good or a bad thing.

The answer should be obvious. Since Pharaoh was converted and ruled as God's representative, bondage to Pharaoh was a species of the liberating bondage of humanity to God. The people were delivered from the horrible bondage of famine and death, the judgment and result of their years of pagan apostasy, and delivered into the hands of a Christian ruler.

Looked at that way, this "enslavement" was a positive thing for that people at that time. We need to ask, however, whether this sets some pattern for the modern world.

Stages of History

To answer that question we need to understand several other factors in the text. If this was just some immediate deliverance, a manifestation of salvation, why did Joseph bind the people to a permanent payment of 20 percent to Pharaoh (Gen. 47:26)? This seems a permanent reduction in status. Perhaps not though. The following observations are pertinent.

First, the Bible teaches that the human race was created to grow through stages, like the stages of growth of the human individual. The entire period of the Old Covenant, from creation to Pentecost, is said to be a time of childhood (Gal. 4:1–3). During this time humanity (including the Jews) was in "bondage" to the "elementary things" (earlier principles) of creation. This "bondage" was a good thing, for the elementary things acted as guardians and tutors to humanity in our infancy

(Gal. 4:1–11). Under the New Covenant men should not go back under this bondage, but under the Old Covenant this kind of bondage was itself a liberating thing.

In other words, there are degrees of liberty. For the Egyptians, to move from bondage to famine into bondage to Pharaoh was a positive step forward. For us to move from our Christian liberty into bondage to the state, however, would be a step backward. History is progressive.

Second, we don't know what kind of situation the Egyptians were in before Joseph enslaved them to Pharaoh. They had to pay 20 percent to Pharaoh thereafter, but possibly this was an improvement over what they had been paying to local lords. The passage does not tell us, but the thrust of the passage is liberation. We may assume some improvement actually took place.

Third, when Pharaoh asked Jacob to bless him, and when he gave the land of Goshen (the best land) to Abraham's children, Pharaoh was submitting to God. The 20 percent tithe was not paid to a purely statist power. A part of that tithe went to the upkeep of the priests of Egypt (also temporarily converted, we may assume) and to the benefit of the priestly nation of Abraham. Possibly we should see the 20 percent as 10 percent for the king and 10 percent for God. At the very least, however, we need to see that the ultimate ruler of Egypt was God Himself, and the ultimate beneficiary of the new tax system was the Church (the priestly nation).

Fourth, the fact that all the land became Pharaoh's, which he then leased out to the people, also sounds bad to us. In the Old Covenant, however, this seems to have been a normal procedure. In Israel, God as King owned all the land, and parcelled it out, establishing regulations for it (cf. e.g., Lev. 25). Among the nations there does not seem to have been any problem with recognizing the king of the nation as God's viceroy in some sense (cf. e.g., Dan. 2:37; 4:25, 32). The pattern of a king's holding the land and leasing it to the people seems to have been part of the "elementary things," seen in Israel as God's owning the land and among the nations as the land owned by the king as God's viceroy. Now that Jesus Christ has been enthroned as King over all the world, we see that He is the one who owns all the land and leases it out to us. It it no longer proper for earthly governments to assume such prerogatives.

Finally, a payment of 20 percent is actually not any kind of enslavement. It is a tax far lower than what modern people pay to our modern statist powers. As Lowenthal asks, "What kind of 'serfdom' is it that grants four-fifths of the produce to the 'serf'?"[2]

What I have been doing in this essay is a "theodicy," a defense of the ways of God to men. We might look at Genesis 47 this way: Pharaoh and Joseph conspired to use the famine as a means of extracting all the capital of Egypt and as a way to reduce the entire population to slavery to a tyrannical state. Such an interpretation, however, goes against every nuance in the text and turns Joseph into a criminal.

What actually happened was this: God brought about the famine as a means of bringing the Egyptian nation to its knees. God converted Pharaoh and the Egyptians. God liberated the Egyptians from bondage and brought them under the rule of a "Christian prince" (Pharaoh) guided by the "Church" (the Hebrews in Goshen). No longer were the Egyptians in psychological bondage to false gods and a static view of history. No longer were they subject to the famine. Now they were free to cultivate the land that God, through Pharaoh and Joseph, gave back to them, provided they gave a double tithe of its produce.

In time, Egypt apostatized. So did the Hebrews. Both repeated the Fall of man, and when that happened the situation became bad once again. In fact, it became worse because of the maturation of humanity (maturation in evil, this time).

[2] E. I. Lowenthal, *The Joseph Narrative in Genesis* (New York: KTAV Pub., 1973), p. 193.

The power of Egypt, built up by the faith and work of Joseph, was turned against God and His people. But that's another story. As the book of Genesis closes, all is well. The book of Genesis ends with a picture of the conversion of the world, a foretaste of the history God has designed for humanity as a whole.

What Genesis 47 describes is a liberation, not an enslavement. It was a step forward in history. It is not, however, a pattern for us to follow today, except in a most general kind of way. The procedures and patterns brought to bear on the situation were part of the "elementary things" of the world, and they have been replaced by the more glorious liberty of the New Covenant. Christ is now our "Pharaoh," our Emperor and Head of the Church, and He requires only a simple 10 percent of us.

Conclusion

All men are slaves. We either serve God or Satan. Back at the beginning, Adam decided to obey Satan, to serve the devil's program instead of God's. Adam volunteered to put himself under another limited creature instead of under the infinite and unlimited Creator. He put himself under a fool instead of under the all-wise God. By doing so he made himself a slave of sin and death. Adam moved from being a son of God to being a son of a beast. Moreover, Adam did not become the son of a domestic beast, but the son of a wild beast (the serpent). He was a threat to God's kingdom—the kind of wild animal that invades God's palace and attacks it and needs to be killed.

Both sons and beasts are slaves, but even domestic beasts are not treated as sons are. Cattle are herded, but sons are treated increasingly as junior partners. Pagan societies, having come under the beast-serpent, always tend toward treating people as cattle. The people exist in "chattel" (cattle) slavery: not a pleasant slavery, but a slavery that leaves them open to all kinds of exploitation and abuse.

Modern man wants to be free of tyranny. We look around
the world at all the people held in slavery by fearful masters,
and we want them to be free. We want to spread democracy
and liberty. But this is a false program, because it is not possible
for men to be totally free. Only God is totally free.

What those held in fearful slavery need is the gospel, which
offers them the opportunity to stop being beasts and start being sons. What men need is not freedom but a new master, the
only true Master. Because the true Master knows how to rule
His sons perfectly, those who become His slaves experience true
freedom and true security and begin to grow toward being junior
partners with Him.

Genesis 47, therefore, is a wonderful presentation of the
gospel. The Egyptians were given the opportunity to break from
being slaves of a pagan lord, slaves of created things like the sun
and the Nile, slaves of Satan. They were given the opportunity
to become slaves of a converted lord, slaves of the God who is
above and outside all limited created things, slaves of "Joseph."
To be sure, they were forced into this move by circumstances
beyond their control. They might have resented it and hated
Joseph. Instead, we find that they rejoiced in their deliverance
and loved Joseph for what he had done for them.

The Egyptians put their faith in the One who provides perfect freedom and security to His servants. May we always do
the same.

SCRIPTURE INDEX

Genesis
1 — 62, 116
1:2 —19
1:2–25 — 13
1:26 — 13, 14
1:28 — 62
1:29 — 62
2 — 21
2:1–3 — 30
2:7 — 45, 56
2:15 — 14
2:16–17 — 61
2:17 — 30
2:18 — 15
2:24 — 81, 142
2:25 — 53
3 — 21
3:6 — 42
3:7 — 53
3:13 — 86
3:15 —
86, 114, 131
3:17–19 — 45
3:18 — 94
3:19 —
31, 45, 81
3:21 — 29
3:24 — 15, 57
4 — 25, 45, 56
4:1–2 — 94
4:3 — 30
4:6 — 55
4:6–7 — 31

4:12 — 45
4:16 — 77
4:23–24 —
32, 41
4:26 — 32
5:21–24 — 33
5:29 — 44
6:1-2 — 41
6:3 — 44
6:5 — 47
6:9 — 51, 93
8 — 95
8:20 — 47
8:21 —
26, 47, 54
9:1 — 56
9:5 — 49
9:5–6 — 41
9:6 — 49
9:20 — 48
9:21 — 48, 51
9:22 — 52, 53
9:23 — 52, 53
9:24 — 54
9:24–25 — 54
10:8–12 — 55
10:13–14 — 135
10:25–30 — 55
11 — 55, 56
11:1 — 55, 58
11:2 — 55, 77
11:3–4 — 56

11:4 — 70
11:5–7 — 57
11:31 — 75
12 — 69,
134, 136
12:1 — 64
12:3 — 136, 137
12:5 — 64
12:6–8 — 64
12:8 — 65, 80
12:10–20 —
65, 76, 89
12:16 — 67
12:16–17 — 87
13:3 — 80
13:4 — 65
13:5–7 — 76
13:8–9 — 77
13:9 — 77
13:10 — 77
13:12 — 77
13:13 — 77
13:18 — 65
14 — 54
14:11–16 — 77
14:13 — 71
14:14 — 71
14:18 — 48, 129
14:19 — 66
14:21 — 71
14:22 — 66
15 — 36, 131

15:1 — 66
15:4 — 67
15:11 — 131
15:13 — 66
16:2 — 67
16:11 — 101
16:16 — 68
17 — 68
17:1 — 68, 93
17:5 — 136
17:17 — 70
17:18–21 — 101
18 71
18:12 — 79
18:14 — 79
18:15 — 79
18:16–22 — 78
18:19 — 69
18:23 — 78
18:27 — 113
18:30-32 — 113
18:32 — 78
19:1 — 79
19:2–3 — 79
19:3 — 79
19:9 — 79
19:16 — 80
19:17 — 80
19:19 — 80
19:19–22 — 80
19:27–28 — 80
19:30 — 81
20 — 89, 135
20:1 — 81
20:2 — 68
20:7 —
    69, 71, 87
20:11 — 68
20:12 — 68, 90

20:14 — 87
20:15 — 69
20:17–18 — 69
20:18 — 68
21:20 — 101
21:12–13 — 101
21:22–34 — 69
22:5 — 70
23 — 72
23:1 — 70
23:6 — 65, 72
23:6–16 — 72
23:12 — 98
23:19 — 81
24 — 95
24:29–31 — 68
24:29–33 — 90
24:50 — 68, 90
24:53 — 90
24:55 — 90
24:55–58 — 95
24:59–60 — 91
24:60 — 68
25:1–7 — 70
25:2–4 — 70
25:19 — 125
25:23 — 93
25:25 — 92
25:26 — 107
25:27 — 93, 94
25:28 — 94, 95
25:29–34 — 94
25:30 — 94
25:34 — 94
26 — 90, 135
26:8–11 — 91
26:12 — 87
26:12–14 — 91
26:15–16 — 92

26:18–20 — 92
26:21 — 92
26:22 — 92
26:23–33 — 92
26:34–35 — 95
27:1 — 96
27:1–5 — 96
27:9 — 96, 125
27:11 — 92
27:12–13 — 96
27:14 — 96
27:15–16 — 96
27:37 — 97
27:40 — 103
27:41–43 — 108
28 — 97
28:1 — 97
28:10–22 — 112
29 — 125
29:14 — 109
29:15 — 109
29:21–30 — 110
29:30–31 — 101
30 — 125
30:25 — 107
30:36 — 110
31:7 — 110
31:15 —
    109, 110
31:17–22 — 110
31:24 — 63, 110
31:26 — 111
31:29 — 110
31:41 —
    107, 109
31:43 — 111
31:44–55 — 111
32:6 — 102, 108
32:9–12 — 112

32:13–20 — 108
32:13–21 — 102
32:22–24 — 107
32:25 — 111
32:25–32 — 114
32:26 —
    113, 116
32:31 — 114
33 — 102
33:3 — 98
33:4 — 103
33:9 — 103
33:9–11 — 102
33:11 — 103
33:12–15 — 102
33:14 — 103
33:28 — 111
34 — 68, 125
35:11 — 124
35:18 — 124
35:28 — 107
36 — 125
36:11 — 102
36:15 — 102
37–50 — 125
37:2 — 117
37:2-3 — 117
37:3 — 117
37:5–11 — 123
37:9–10 — 98
37:14 — 117
37:18 — 120
37:18–19 — 122
37:21–28 — 117
37:23 — 117
37:26 — 122
37:31 — 104
37:35 — 125
38:17–20 — 104

39:1 — 119
39:1–7 — 117
39:3 — 118
39:4 — 118
39:6 — 118
39:7–12 — 118
39:12–18 — 118
39:19 — 119
39:20 — 119
39:20–23 — 118
40 — 11, 130
40:2 — 129
40:3 — 119
40:14–15 — 121
40:23 — 121
41 — 130, 137
41:1 — 121
41:1–8 — 132
41:6 — 134
41:8–9 — 130
41:16 — 121
41:25 — 121
41:28 — 121
41:32 — 121
41:37 — 135
41:38 —
    135, 137
41:39–40 — 135
41:40 —
    119, 139
41:41 — 139
41:42 —
    119, 139
41:45 — 135
41:46 — 107
41:46–57 — 139
41:57 —
    119, 137
42:1 — 125

42:2 — 125
42:8–16 — 120
42:15–17 — 120
42:17 — 120
42:18 — 121
42:18–20 — 126
42:21 — 120
42:36 —
    125, 126
42:37 — 126
43:1–14 — 125
43:8 — 126
43:9 — 124
43:14 — 126
43:23 — 136
43:32 — 123
43:33 — 123
43:34 — 121
44:2 — 123, 139
44:4–6 — 122
44:5 —
    122, 130, 139
44:12 — 139
44:15 — 123
44:16-17 — 139
44:17 — 121
44:18–34 — 124
45:8 —
    70, 119, 136
44:9 — 121
44:33 — 122

45:16 — 136
45:17–20 — 136
45:22 — 122
45:27 — 126
47 —
    141, 147, 148, 149
47:7 — 136

47:9 — 107
47:10 — 136
47:25 — 144
47:26 — 145
49:10 — 124
49:29–32 — 101
50:3 — 136
50:7 — 136

Exodus
1:20 — 87
2 — 86
3:13–15 — 116
20:2 — 124
20:10–11 — 18
21 — 144
22:3 — 121
23:19 — 104
33:18–23 — 116
33:19 — 65
33:20 — 116
34:26 — 104
34:5 — 65
34:5–7 — 116

Leviticus
19:26 — 123
25 — 146

Numbers
12:6–8 — 116
23:23 — 123
32:12 — 102

Deuteronomy
1:39 — 62
2:22 — 102
3:16 — 107
14:21 — 104

14:26 — 48
21:17 — 96

Joshua
2 — 87
12:2 — 107
14:6 — 102
14:14 — 102
15:17 — 102
24:2 — 75
24:4 — 102

Judges
1:13 — 102
3:9 — 102
3:11 — 102
4 — 87
5 — 87
5:24 — 87
5:31 — 114
8:4 — 114
8:13 — 114
8:22 — 124
9 — 45, 94
9:13 — 48
15:1 — 104

2 Samuel
12 — 88
12:13–15 — 87
13 — 68
14 — 88
14:17 — 63
16:2 — 87
19:20 — 63
19:27 — 63
19:35 — 63
24:4–6 — 64

1 Kings
3 — 63
3:9 — 63

2 Kings
6:28 — 104

1 Chronicles
4:15 — 102

Nehemiah
1:11 — 130
2:1 — 130

Esther
2:10 — 98
2:20 — 98
3:2 — 98

Job
1:1 — 93, 102
2:11 — 102
27:4 — 55
33:3 — 55

Psalms
1 — 45, 94
8:3-4 — 18
8:5 — 49
8:5-6 — 18
12:2–4 — 55
16:4 — 55
34 — 87
34:8 — 34
40:9 — 55
45:2 — 55
51:15 — 55
81:5 — 55
104:15 — 48

127 — 70
139:22 — 101

Proverbs
  6:6-8 — 15
  8:35–36 — 42
  22:7 — 121

Song of Solomon
  4:9 — 90
  4:10 — 90
  4:12 — 90
  5:1 — 90
  5:2 — 90
  8:8 — 90

Isaiah
  6:3 — 37
  6:5 — 55
  6:7 — 55
  19:18 — 55
  61:1–2 — 137

Lamentations
  4:10 — 104
  4:21 — 102

Ezekiel
  14:14–20 — 51
  28:13-14 — 16

Daniel
  2:37 — 146
  4 — 99, 135
  4:25 — 146
  4:32 — 146

Amos
  3:7 — 71
  7:2–3 — 71
  7:5–6 — 71

Zephaniah
  2:8–10 — 82
  3:9 — 55

Malachi
  1:26 — 101
  2:6–7. — 55

Matthew
  1:5 — 87
  5:41 — 85
  6:33 — 65
  7:17–19 — 45
  10:16 — 86
  11:11 — 116
  22:30 — 90
  23:31 — 31
  23:33 — 86
  23:35 — 31
  25:14–30 — 143

Mark
  10:42–45 — 117

Luke
  1:71 — 124
  1:74 — 124
  1:75 — 124
  3:38 — 14
  4 — 137
  4:16–30 — 137
  4:18–19 — 137

4:21 — 137
4:22 — 138
4:23–27 — 138
4:28–30 — 138
14:7–11 — 72
14:26 — 101
15:20 — 103
16:16 — 113
24 — 88

John
  8:44 — 86
  14–17 — 34

Acts
  2 — 59

Romans
  1:18–32 — 58
  1:21 — 22
  1:21–23 — 26
  2 — 137
  3 — 137
  8:19–22 — 36
  9:13 — 101
  9:14 — 101
  12:19 — 43
  13:1–7 — 85
  13:4 — 43

2 Corinthians
  3:18 — 116
  5:21 — 30
  11:3 — 86

Galatians
  4:1–3 — 145
  4:1–11 — 146

4:21–31 — 101
6:16 — 114

Ephesians
2:6 — 116
2:8–10 — 23
6:5–8 — 127

Colossians
1:13–23 — 36

1 Thessalonians
5:18 — 38

1 Timothy
2:2 — 85
2:14 — 86

Hebrews
2:8 — 61
2:10 — 61
4:12 — 36
5:1 — 63
5:4 — 63
5:10 — 63
5:14 — 63
6 — 61
6:12–15 — 61
6:12–18 — 61
9:7 — 116
10:19–22 — 116
11 — 61
11:7 — 44
11:9–10 — 82
11:20 — 97
12 — 61
12:16–17 — 101

James
2:18 — 23
2:25 — 87
3:16 — 76
3:17 — 77
5:16 — 69

1 Peter
2:4–8 — 56
3:20 — 44

2 Peter
2:5 — 44
2:7 — 75

Jude
14–15 — 33
16 — 33

Revelation
1:16 — 114
4:8 — 37
7:9 — 59